GROUNDING KNOWLEDGE

Environmental

Philosophy,

Epistemology,

and Place

GROUNDING KNOWLEDGE

Christopher J. Preston

The University of Georgia Press
Athens and London

Published by the University of Georgia Press

Athens, Georgia 30602

© 2003 by Christopher J. Preston

Designed by Jennifer Smith

Set in 10.2/13.5 Minion by Bookcomp, Inc.

Printed and bound by Maple-Vail

The paper in this book meets the guidelines for
permanence and durability of the Committee on
Production Guidelines for Book Longevity of the
Council on Library Resources.

Printed in the United States of America

07 06 05 04 03 C 5 4 3 2 1

Library of Congress Cataloging-in-Publication Data

Preston, Christopher J.

Grounding knowledge : environmental philosophy,

epistemology, and place / Christopher J. Preston.

        p.   cm.

Includes bibliographical references and index.

ISBN 0-8203-2450-7 (alk. paper)

1. Knowledge, Theory of.   2. Environmentalism—
Philosophy.   I. Title.

BD161 .P746 2003

121—dc21   2002011505

British Library Cataloging-in-Publication Data available

To my family.

For staying so close,
while so far away.

Contents

Acknowledgments

I would like to express my sincere gratitude to the following people for having given their time—in some cases an awful lot of it—to improve the shape of this manuscript: Nancy Tuana, Mark Johnson, Louise Westling, Scott Pratt, Irene Diamond, Davis Baird, Anne Bezuidenhout, Jan Opsomer, Thomas Lekan, R. I. G. Hughes, Jason Kawall, Jennifer Hollis, and David Strohmaier. Most of these people have done far more for me at different points during this process as critics and as friends than the mere mention of their names can convey. My debt is deep and my appreciation immense. I would also like to thank Barbara Ras at the University of Georgia Press for being a friendly, helpful, and accessible editor.

I would like to express a different kind of gratitude to the following people for having given me standards to aspire to in the way that I write and think about philosophy and the environment: to Holmes Rolston III for showing how to think critically and to write lyrically, to David Abram for showing how to insert creativity and a little magic into academic spaces, and to Julie Belknap for showing how to consistently bring natural wonder(s) into the very fiber of one's being.

I would also like to thank the late Toby Rilling and Scott Allee for having helped create opportunities for me to spend large amounts of time in Alaska and for having shared many of those times with me there.

Finally, since this book is about the influence of place on how we think about the world, I must offer perhaps my deepest gratitude to a few of the places that I believe have most affected the way that I think. The South Downs in East Sussex, England, will in some sense always be my home. The chalk and flint of the footpaths that cross those gentle hills is permanently inscribed on the soles of my boots. The Five Valleys area around Missoula, Montana—especially the Rattlesnake Valley—have offered many miles of river, path, and forest for my exploration. The wildflowers, black bears, and oxygen-sucking climbs that those places afford continue to be fertile ground for my mental cultivation. Finally, Prince William Sound in Alaska has on many occasions injected enlivening geological and ecological drama into my soul. The sea lions and bald eagles, the humpback whales and the pink salmon, have all left a mark on me. I will never forget these environments, and I am glad of this opportunity to thank them.

INTRODUCTION

This is a book about the connections between place and mind. It describes how our physical environment comes to play an important role in structuring the way we think. I argue that organisms that know things about the world are situated beings, beings cognitively grounded in the worlds from which they speak. An important part of this grounding is a physical location among material realities such as mountains and freeways, oceans and apartment buildings, trees and automobiles, factories and crowds. These physical things lend shape to mental activity. They comprise some of the important factors relevant to how we know.

To give this book an academic location, it is a work in postmodern epistemology. It is "epistemology" because it is a study of what is going on when we claim to know something about the world. It is "postmodern" because it builds upon work in the late twentieth century that began to unravel modernist views of how we know the world. One version of this unraveling is told in the first chapter. Although the book claims a postmodern location, I articulate a version of postmodernism that is deeply ambivalent about some of the signature claims of the movement. In particular, a large part of the point of this book is to show that postmodernists have unwittingly retained one of the critical weaknesses of the view they intended to supersede. This critical weakness is a form of human-centeredness that can usefully be called "anthropocentrism."

Anthropocentrism is an overemphasis on the centrality of human values and concerns at the expense of nonhuman ones. In ethics, anthropocentrists maintain that humans are the primary—and often the only—centers of value in the world. They deny that anything nonhuman has any value in itself. Non-anthropocentric ethicists, by contrast, regard nonhuman nature as a source of its own value. In epistemology, anthropocentrists likewise are guilty of neglecting the nonhuman world when they offer critical analyses of why thought and belief take the particular shape they do. Anthropocentrists consider only human-centered social factors for explaining the shape of our knowledge claims. A non-anthropocentric epistemology such as the one articulated in this book, like a non-anthropocentric ethic, looks beyond simply social and cultural factors when trying to answer the question of why knowledge is shaped the way it is. Such an epistemology insists that the physical realities of the environments in which beliefs are formed are relevant to the ways people know. It refuses to let knowledge float free of its connections to our embodied and embedded nature in the physical world. In short, a non-anthropocentric epistemology tethers thinking, knowing, and believing to some rich and earthbound material roots.

There are at least two reasons why this is a good time to talk about grounding knowledge and belief in the earth. From the point of view of intellectual fashion, there has been a flurry of recent work in the philosophy of mind, epistemology, and the philosophy of science showing how the human mind and the thought processes in which it engages are much more integrated into the material realities of the world than had been previously thought. Although it used to be claimed that thinking and believing literally lift us out of our bodies, fully detaching us from our cell processes, cultural backgrounds, and organismic locations in the world, many contemporary positions describe mental activity that is grounded in nonnegotiably worldly contexts. These worldly contexts in the first instance have included the structures of the social and academic communities in which knowledge producers operate. But it has recently become much more common to think that our beliefs are also influenced by the physical details of the brain, the body, the laboratory, and the urban landscape. The old idea that humans might have access to a fully detached and Godlike view from above is now regarded in many quarters with suspicion. As a result of these intellectual currents, those who study epistemology have become much more prepared to look at human knowledge as a situated phenomenon, tied in subtle ways to the places and times in which it operates. The trend is toward situating thought and belief and granting to the mind a variety of constitutive ties to the different worlds in which it operates. Finding out what is involved in situating thought in its earthly contexts is certainly a delicate and complex task. The work is contentious and provocative at times, but I believe it has an important political dimension. This is a politics that can be conciliatory, empowering, and ultimately liberatory in a number of ways. I hope this book contains a small portion of that work.

A second reason why this is a good time to talk about grounding knowledge has more to do with the goals of environmentalists than with contemporary intellectual trends in epistemology. As photographs from space make startlingly clear, humans are located on a deeply blue, infinitely complex, and—so far—apparently unique, verdant planet that supplies the conditions and possibilities for absolutely everything we do. It is clear that, in some sense, the earth is literally the ground for all our knowledge claims. For the vast majority of species for the vast majority of their time, the earth has been the place from which they know.[1] What those same images from space have also made abundantly clear is that each and every heady debate about postmodernism and epistemology takes place against the background of the systematic impoverishment of many of those biotic systems in the face of increasing populations and consumption patterns. It is now well understood that these consumption patterns come at the cost of a significant loss of the planet's cultural and biological diversity.

Since traditional discussions of knowledge have generally assumed that human situatedness in a physical environment is not relevant to matters of the mind, this continuing impoverishment of the natural environment has rarely been considered to have any detrimental effect on thought and belief. Epistemologists theorizing about knowledge might be vaguely concerned that a biologically impoverished planet could adversely affect their nutrition and their respiration, but they have never suggested that it might also adversely affect their decision and their contemplation. In the accounts of thought and mind that we have inherited in Western philosophy, the accepted story is that environmental destruction affects biology but not epistemology.

This book challenges that traditional account. As creatures who survive only because we are situated in delicate ecological relationships with the world around us, humans now generally recognize that we are connected at a biological level to the systems around us. Clearly it is in our own biological interest to treat natural systems with care. I argue that humans, as creatures with minds operating through ongoing and active relationships with our physical environments, are also profoundly connected *at a psychological level* to our historical, biological, and geographical situation on this planet. This means it is not only in our biological interest but also *in our cognitive interest* to protect these connections. For it is in these contexts that the human mind operates.

Before starting the argument for grounding knowledge, I want to briefly indicate what could be gained from this endeavor. Coming back down to earth about knowledge and belief is, I believe, one of the steps necessary for creating less destructive kinds of attitudes between humans and their natural environments. Humans have for too long thought that knowledge lifts them out of their world. Environmentalists, both inside and outside of the academic setting, can profit from the suggestion made by Paul Shepard a quarter of a century ago that there is "a strange and necessary relationship between place and mind."[2]

Inside the academy, grounding knowledge has significant implications for environmental philosophy. Officially sanctioned as a genuine branch of philosophy for barely twenty-five years, environmental philosophy currently gazes upon numerous unexplored avenues of inquiry. Subversive by its nature, it holds license to challenge some of Western philosophy's most entrenched dogmas. Connecting the structures of thought and mind more closely to the earth can begin to undo one of the philosophical canon's most pernicious conceptual divisions. From virtually the earliest utterances in the Western philosophical tradition, humans have differentiated themselves from—and elevated themselves above—the rest of nature on the basis of their supposedly unique capacity to use reason. Something about this ability has been assumed a priori to mark a point of severance between humans and everything non-human. Grounding knowledge offers a direct challenge to this by suggesting that there are deep connections between, on the one hand, the rational mind and the beliefs it forms and, on the other, the nonhuman, physical realities of our environments. This makes the capacity to reason and form beliefs considerably less of a point of departure than it currently appears. If reason is structurally wedded to the physical geographies of the earth, then we have little justification for thinking that it is sufficient to elevate us above all the non-human parts of nature. At the very least, the position provides environmental philosophers with an additional reason to value the physical environments in which thought operates.

Outside of the academy, claims like Shepard's are also suggestive for how they might add considerable substance to the popular notion of a "sense of place." Environmentalists have recently become fond of saying that the redis-covery of a sense of place is an important tool for beginning to bring human communities back into a more responsible set of relationships with the earth. As the environmental message percolated through different groups in the late twentieth century, the early slogan "think globally, act locally" was gradually transformed into the more intimate and powerful injunction to renew and revive for ourselves a strong sense of place. Environmentalists have begun to think that personal attachments to particular landscapes are at the heart of environmental action. Aldo Leopold overstated it a little, perhaps, but clearly captured something important when he claimed, "We can be ethical only in relationship to something we can see, feel, understand, love, or otherwise have faith in."[3]

Different people have called this process of achieving a sense of place differ-ent things. Gary Snyder, for example, called it "the real work" of reinhabita-tion. Wes Jackson called it "becoming native" to a place.[4] While few who hear this phrase appear to have any trouble getting a vague idea of what a sense of place is—a kind of warm and nostalgic feeling toward the places in which they feel at home—it has usually proven hard to say anything concrete about why people actually have this feeling of being tied to particular places. It has been hard to articulate the kind of mechanisms that might operate to create a sense of place. Shepard's proposed connection between place and mind starts to suggest some answers. If he was right about the links between place and mind, then the very cognitive processes with which we contemplate our place in the world are themselves *derived from* and *wedded to* our physical located-ness. This claim entails that part of the feeling of attachment to place is quite literally an attachment of a portion of our cognitive architecture to the lands we inhabit. Paula Gunn Allen once remarked that for her community to lose their land is equivalent to them losing their minds.[5] Such statements have proved to be effective rallying cries for diverse groups of environmental and social justice activists. Shepard's suggestions, and others like them that I offer in this book, are important parts of the evidence for why Allen's remark is not as strange as it initially sounds.

The argument of this book takes the following form. Chapter 1 sets up the problem by sketching how the view that thought and belief are detached from the physical environment became so central in Western philosophy. I discuss two occasions on which this detached view ran into significant problems and a solution that was offered on each occasion. These proposed solutions indicate a possible common path that can be taken back toward reattaching knowledge and belief to the physical environment. Chapter 2 details a range of contemporary work in the philosophy of science, epistemology, and cognitive science by theorists who have already begun to move us down that path. Chapter 3 reaches a little more widely across the disciplines to support the view that this is the right path to take. I show how particular approaches to biology, ecological psychology, and the philosophy of mind all require us to re-emphasize the significance of physical environments to matters of mind. In chapter 4, I start to focus the argument for environmentalists by bringing this evidence to bear specifically on natural environments. I illustrate some of the points of the previous chapters with a narrative discussion of some of my own epistemic experiences in a particularly dramatic natural environment. I also include in chapter 4 a discussion of the Western Apache moral system as a helpful illustration of how physical environments can structure a local belief system.[6] In chapter 5, I take a position on why these ideas are significant both for contemporary epistemology and for contemporary environmental philosophy. In chapter 6, I argue for a specific recommendation for environmental policymakers and activists based on the connections between place and mind I have articulated.

The particular track I take toward these conclusions is gloriously idiosyncratic. As someone shaped by body, culture, and environment, I make no claim to have any kind of privileged perspective from which to make this case. The people I have met and have been influenced by, the books I have read, the places and experiences that have made me think about these things the way that I do constitute a personal history that readers are largely spared. Similar conclusions could no doubt be reached using different figures and by piecing the story together in dramatically different ways. What follows is neither the best nor the only way to make this case. But having made this disclaimer, I add that I am not entirely convinced that making the single most airtight case has to be the *only* goal for those—like myself—who identify themselves as environmentalists. Toward the end of his award-winning book on how the creation of the alphabet subtly influenced how we treat the earth, David Abram suggested that "to explain is not to present a set of finished reasons, but to tell a story. . . . [This] is an unfinished story, told from various angles, sketchy in some parts, complete with gaps and questions and unrealized characters. But it is a story, nonetheless, not a wholly determinate set of facts. . . . [A] story must be judged according to whether it *makes sense*. And 'making sense' here must be understood in its most direct meaning: to make sense is to *enliven the senses*. . . . To *make sense* is to release the body from the constraints imposed by outworn ways of speaking, and hence to renew and rejuvenate one's felt awareness of the world. It is to make the senses wake up to where they are." [7] I offer what follows in the same spirit as Abram offers his work. If this story makes sense, then I hope it will contribute to a body of work that seeks to reawaken us to how the physical spaces around us are deeply woven into the fabric of who we are. This weaving, I argue, occurs at both a biological and a cognitive level. Not only does every cell in our body ultimately draw its atoms and its energy from the world around us; so does every thought and belief depend ultimately for its structure on the ways in which we are grounded by our physical environments. This is a provocative suggestion. It is one that I hope can both humble and inspire.

GROUNDING KNOWLEDGE

Places are important because all we really have are our particular places, our localities. We do not live in the universal, only in our small portions of the universe.

Sherman Paul, "From Here/Now: Mostly on Place"

1 UNNATURAL KNOWLEDGE

Twenty years ago, Paul Shepard broke new ground by publishing a number of provocative books exploring the links between the natural environments in which humans evolved and the social, cultural, and intellectual structures that make balanced and creative thought possible. In *Nature and Madness,* Shepard claimed that the important formative relationship between the infant and primary caregiver is itself situated relative to another equally important series of relationships. He observed that over evolutionary time, caregiving had taken place in the middle of "a surround of living plants, rich in texture, smell, and motion. The unfiltered, unpolluted air, the flicker of wild birds, real sunshine and rain, mud to be tasted and tree bark to grasp, the sounds of wind and water, the calls of animals and insects as well as human voices—all these are not vague and pleasant amenities for the infant, but the stuff out of which its second grounding, even while in its mother's arms, has begun. The outdoors is also in some sense another inside, a kind of enlivenment of that fetal landscape. . . . The surroundings are also that-which-will-be-swallowed, internalized, incorporated as the self."[1] Shepard believed that the physical geography and the biological diversity accompanying early childhood supplied a critical grounding for the development of mind. He worried that contemporary alienation from traditional childhood experiences in nature risked causing us various sorts of cognitive harm. Our systems of thought had emerged out of particular kinds of landscapes and the activities we historically practiced there. Dissociating ourselves from those familiar places in nature would yield a certain kind of madness.

Although it was certainly provocative, Shepard's thesis about nature and madness always hovered around the fringes of respectability. Despite a significant number of readers who admired the breadth and daring of his vision, others rejected the idea that anything about environment could possibly be important to matters of mind. His work remained a little too controversial, a little too interdisciplinary, and, frankly, a little too difficult to read—moving at breathtaking speed between biology, anthropology, theology, poetics, and psychology—ever to pass wide critical muster. Shepard frequently inspired, but his work remained marginal. An additional barrier to the broad acceptance of his work was that when Shepard was at the peak of his productivity there were no suitable disciplines available to house his odd-sounding remarks about the intertwining of place and mind. Neither epistemology nor empirical studies of mind nor the philosophy of science had prepared any such ground. Environmental philosophy barely existed, ecopsychology still lay some years in the future, and only a few environmental studies programs were up and running. His suggestions about how thought and mind were tied into the physical environment often read like a form of slightly misfitted, paleolithic romanticism. Nobody in academic circles wanted to claim them as their own.

But pioneers cut paths that others can follow. Two decades later, the situation has significantly changed. There is now considerably more ground prepared to house those provocative claims about the relationship between place and mind. In this first chapter, I begin to explore some of that ground. Unlike Shepard, my own claims are not directed toward any conception of human mental health. I have nothing at all to suggest about the causes of madness, but what I have to say has a strong resonance with Shepard's view that mind and world coexist in a much tighter relationship than has been appreciated in the past. My position is that the physical world offers irreplaceable assistance to mind in the work it does. Thought, knowledge, and belief are not products of mind alone but expressions of its integration and participation with the physical world that lies around it. Recognition of this cooperative relationship brings human knowledge firmly back down to earth.

To make such radical claims flies in the face of most of the history of Western philosophy. It challenges one of our most entrenched dogmas about there being a clear separation between the products of reason and the products of nature. In order to set the scene for the argument for grounding knowledge, it is necessary first to consider how and why it left the ground in the first place. This involves a somewhat lengthy excursus into the ideas of a few of the philosophers who have most shaped Western philosophy's opinions about thought and belief, an excursus necessary in order to plot a way around the philosophical dogma we have inherited.

Disconnecting Place and Mind

Few would argue with the most general claim that humans blend their sense experience with their reasoning powers to form beliefs about the world. But when it comes to saying a little more about what it means to reason and what actually goes into the construction of those beliefs, things rapidly get much more difficult. How does the human mind come to create its descriptions of the world? How do we know when our beliefs are true? What sort of an entity is knowledge? What is the relationship between beliefs held in the mind and facts residing in the world? The discussion becomes so complex so quickly that philosophy devoted a whole area of inquiry to sorting through these topics. The study of epistemology—a study in Bertrand Russell's words into the "limits and scope of knowledge"—is that inquiry.

Like so many of the central philosophical inquiries, the origins of Western epistemology are traceable to ancient Greece. Twenty-four hundred years ago, an aristocratic and curious young man named Plato, reveling in the heady discussions of post-Periclean Athens, scribbled down some fairly detailed accounts of the arguments that he heard. He later supplemented these reports with his own fictional dialogues on various topics of philosophical interest to him. Plato advanced most of his philosophical speculations through the mouthpiece of Socrates, a much loved but stubborn and often controversial presence in Athens. Socrates was eventually brought to trial for corrupting the youth and for not believing in the city's gods. But this was not before he had spent most of his life making the case that knowledge was something that must be identified and separated from mere opinion. As Socrates shaped the contours of this distinction, knowledge first began to leave the ground.

Socrates began his defense speech at his trial by paying characteristic false homage to those against whom he argued. He continued by asserting that there was an important distinction to be made between truth and simply good rhetoric.

I do not know what effect my accusers have had upon you, gentlemen, but for my own part I was almost carried away by them—their arguments were so convincing. On the other hand, scarcely a word of what they said was true. . . . I have not the slightest skill as a speaker—unless, of course, by skillful speaker they mean one who speaks the truth. . . . [F]rom me you will hear the whole truth—not, I can assure you, gentlemen, in flowery language like theirs, decked out with fine words and phrases. No, what you will hear will be a straightforward speech in the first words that occur to me, confident as I am in the justice of my cause.[2]

By the time his well-connected and eloquent biographer Plato had chronicled the events that followed in graphic and often heroic detail, the debate about the nature of truth and knowledge had suddenly become very important indeed. "What is knowledge?" and "What is the distinction between truth and opinion?" became philosophy's foundational questions. With Socrates as midwife, epistemology had been born.

Alfred North Whitehead once famously remarked that all of philosophy is a footnote to Plato. Once a philosophical idea has been effectively articulated it often holds its power for centuries. The Platonic account of knowledge is a case in point. Important roots of the contemporary disconnection of place and mind can be found right here. Plato articulated through Socrates a position according to which knowledge resides in a location far removed from our everyday lives and activities. In his allegory of the cave, Socrates suggested to Glaucon that gaining knowledge involved a long and arduous struggle to climb up out of the darkness of the cave in which we spend most of our lives and into the light of a very different kind of world. Discovering truth meant using rational powers to ascend to a completely separate realm of existence. This separate realm was located above the everyday appearances of the world. The difference between mere opinion and knowledge was the difference between being stuck in the cave watching shadows and escaping out of the cave and into the light in order to see things that were real. Knowledge dealt with objects much more sharp, much more enduring, and much more real than any of the shadows and illusions of the everyday world. "[I]f you assume that the ascent and the contemplation of the things above is the soul's ascension to the intelligible region," Socrates counseled Glaucon, "you will not miss my surmise."[3]

This metaphor of knowledge as a form of ascent away from the shadowy and confusing particulars of the everyday world was articulated again in the *Symposium*. Here Socrates described in detail the process of gaining knowledge of beauty by recounting a speech given to him by Diotima, a priestess from the city of Mantineia. Diotima explained how gaining knowledge of beauty meant using different individuals "like rising stairs" to abstract a general idea of beauty from the particular examples of beauty embodied in individuals. Diotima described in detail how a person wishing to know beauty should proceed. "[F]irst . . . he should love one body and beget beautiful ideas there; then he should realize that the beauty of any one body is brother to the beauty of any other and that if he is to pursue beauty of form, he'd be very foolish not to think that the beauty of all bodies is one and the same. When he grasps this, he must become a lover of all beautiful bodies, and he must think that this wild gaping after just one body is a small thing and despise it."[4] In the view that Diotima described, knowing essentially became a matter of progressively abstracting away from the physical. It required moving away from the specificities of particular flesh-and-blood individuals. To gain knowledge of beauty, the mind must grasp something abstract.[5] The beauty of particular flesh-and-blood individuals had to be left behind because knowledge was by definition the knowledge of something universal, and there was nothing universal to be found within any single, corruptible piece of physical matter.

Successfully ascending the ladder in order to know beauty signified the ability to use reason to rise above all the idiosyncrasies that taint particular examples of beauty to achieve knowledge of beauty itself. Such knowledge, in Plato's terminology, was knowledge of the "form" of beauty. The forms were actual nonphysical entities, similar in some ways to numbers, from which all other appearances were derived. Knowledge of these forms came with a set of distinctive qualities. Diotima said of the form of beauty: "first, it always is and neither comes to be nor passes away . . . second it is not beautiful this way and ugly that way, nor beautiful at one time and ugly at another. . . . [I]t is not anywhere in another thing, as in an animal, or in earth, or in heaven, or in anything else but itself by itself with itself, it is always one in form."[6] Knowledge of the forms is, in other words, eternal, universal, and nonmaterial. In the *Timaeus,* Plato confirmed this when he announced: "That which is apprehended by intelligence and reason is always in the same state, but that which is conceived by opinion with the help of sensation and without reason is always in a process of becoming and perishing and never really is."[7] There is a permanence and something that can usefully start to be characterized as a "hyper-purity" to knowledge that made its strict isolation from the physical world a matter of necessity for Plato. In Plato's hands, knowledge had begun to detach itself from the earth. It had started to have little connection to the world in which we taste, breathe, and live the sensuous parts of our lives.

These themes of detachment from the physical world are largely consistent throughout Plato's dialogues. The "divided line" described in the *Republic* offers a schema for how knowledge differed from mere opinion. The former was found not in any of the material or physical realities of the visible world but in the pure and abstract realities of the intelligible world accessible only through reason. In the *Phaedrus,* Plato asserted of the disembodied world in which knowledge was found that "[I]t is there that true being dwells, without color or shape, that cannot be touched; reason alone, the soul's pilot, can behold it, and all true knowledge is knowledge thereof."[8] With knowledge so abstracted from the world, the intrusion of the body took on negative connotations. In the *Phaedo,* Socrates characterized the body as an impediment to a person's efforts to gain knowledge. He described the necessity of a process of purification through which the lover of learning must go in order to prepare for knowledge. The process consisted of "separating the soul as much as possible from the body and accustoming it to withdraw from all contact with the body and concentrate itself by itself, and to have its dwelling, so far as it can, both now and in the future, alone by itself, freed from the shackles of the body."[9] Through this transcending of the body and the rest of the material world, Plato thought that a person might participate in something divine rather than earthly. He claimed that the person who succeeded in attaining knowledge "grows wings . . . [and] stands outside human concerns and draws close to the divine; ordinary people think he is disturbed and rebuke him for this, unaware that he is possessed by god."[10]

Plato's early characterization of what was involved in gaining knowledge set some important ground rules. Knowledge was abstract rather than particular, timeless rather than temporally bounded, divine rather than human, and ideal rather than embodied. Knowledge was about grasping universal truths, good for all time. It meant transcending human limits. It required disengaging from everything about us that is human and physical and using reason—a gift from the gods—as a conduit back up toward truths located somewhere else entirely. All of these ground rules made knowledge into something hyper-pure, unpolluted by the messy physicality and particularity of earthly matters.

The rather odd implication of all this was that human knowledge required systematically excluding everything distinctively human about the knowledge maker. The contingencies of the human body and the different situations in which the body found itself were regarded not as contributions but as impediments to knowledge. Once these impediments had been overcome, there was in truth no longer any way to characterize knowledge as distinctively *human* knowledge at all. Knowledge was possible for humans only if they left their humanity behind. Epistemology had been given its direction, and this direction was emphatically away from particulars of the body, from the human considered as a whole organism, and from any of the details of the physical environments within which that human might dwell. Knowledge, in short, had lost its grounding.

Though the story of the cave was only an allegory and the ideas contained in it only metaphors, the broad contours of Plato's account of knowledge held extraordinary power. This was true even for those who disagreed with it. Aristotle almost immediately challenged Plato's view that the objects of knowledge belonged in a completely different sphere. Considerably more worldly and practical in orientation than Plato, Aristotle denied both the coherence and the usefulness of a whole separate world of the forms. But having quickly dropped Plato's separate world of the forms, Aristotle went ahead and retained other aspects of the Platonic account. For knowledge to be possible, Aristotle still insisted that the mind should be "capable of receiving the form of an object."[11] The form, redesigned in certain ways so that it could exist in objects themselves rather than in a separate world, had to be grasped in order for something to be known. The form still had a universality to it that meant it had to be something distinct from the physical object itself.

In addition to retaining the view that knowing an object meant knowing its form, Aristotle also retained the belief that the process of knowing does not in any way depend upon, nor is it structured by, any of the physical specificities of our bodies. The physical parts of our bodies had many other important roles to play, but they did not have any influence on producing the shape of knowledge. Knowing demanded of mind that it have complete flexibility to assume the form that was brought by the object of knowledge. The part of us that knows, Aristotle contended, "cannot reasonably be regarded as blended with any part of the body."[12] Only a particular kind of hyper-purity would provide the mind with the flexibility required to take up the form of any object. In order to know, Aristotle claimed, the mind must be "pure from all admixture . . . for the co-presence of what is alien to its nature is a hindrance and a block."[13] Nearly two thousand years later, Shakespeare elegantly characterized this purity of mind as its "glassy essence." Knowledge of something physical ironically had to be completely unconstrained by anything physical for it to be possible at all.

These views had staying power. Through the works of neo-Platonic and Arabic commentators, and later through direct translation of Aristotelian texts, the contours of this epistemology reappeared throughout the Western philosophical tradition. Medieval epistemology in Europe was fundamentally Aristotelian with strong neo-Platonic influences. The ocular metaphor of light and darkness established by Plato remained central through several philosophical schools. The idea that knowing meant illuminating truth with the help of a divine light passed through Augustine and St. Thomas Aquinas and on into the modern epistemologies of both John Locke and René Descartes. Importing the ancient idea of knowledge as a kind of illumination and giving it a Christian spin, Locke described reason as "the candle of the Lord set up by himself in men's minds."[14] Descartes also spoke of the "light of reason" that made possible "clear and distinct ideas."[15] At the birth of the modern age in philosophy, achieving knowledge still involved getting out of the darkness of the cave and into the light.

Other Platonic themes also remained. The same Greek word that Plato had used for form was also used in modern epistemology to describe what the mind grasps when it has knowledge. The forms of Plato were transliterated into the "ideas" of Descartes and Locke. Locke designated "idea" to stand for "whatsoever is the Object of the Understanding when a Man thinks."[16] Descartes had a similar view in which "idea" referred to "whatever is imme- diately perceived by the mind."[17] For both thinkers, ideas were the things on which the rational human mind carried out its operations. For empiricists such as Locke, only after the acquisition of an idea through sense experience did the understanding have anything in front of it to work upon. For rational- ists such as Descartes, some of these ideas could be found in the mind prior to any sensory experience of the world.

This conversion of forms into ideas brought with it most of the Greek as- sumptions about the detachment of knowledge from the world. Though there was no longer a separate realm of the forms, Locke and Descartes retained the commitment to the hyper-purity of things held by the mind. Both still believed that ideas were necessarily immaterial and disembodied. The hyper-purity of ideas demanded that there still be a significant distinction between the kind of thing knowledge was and the kind of things that knowledge was about. The moderns achieved this with what today appears to be a much more intuitively appealing story than the one Plato had told. In Descartes's hands, the mind be- came a radically different kind of substance from the body. Whereas the body was made up of extended substance, the mind was made up of an entirely dif- ferent thinking substance. Knowledge no longer depended for its universality on grasping a form located in some strangely elevated Platonic realm, nor did it require an elusive Aristotelian essence of an object. Its universality was made possible by the fact that it was a product of an immaterial mind made up of a substance completely transcending the materiality of the human body.

Treating the mind as wholly separate substance also meant that knowing be- came a slightly different process in the modern period.[18] For Aristotle, when the mind knew the shape of a tree, it had literally been imprinted with the form of the tree. But the ideas of the moderns were not literally impressed upon the glassy essence of the mind as they had been for the ancients. They were placed *in front of it* like an image on a screen. The modern picture assumed that the mind possessed something like an inner eye of its own that operated separately from the eyes of the body. This inner eye could look upon the different simple and complex ideas that appeared in front of it and make knowledge claims about them. Truth and falsity lay in judgments of correspondence between the ideas and the world. Knowledge occurred when the mind made a correct judgment that the ideas it saw with its inner eye accurately *represented* something in the world outside. For Descartes, knowledge of physical objects consisted in "my judging that the ideas which are in me resemble, or conform to, things located outside me."[19] For Locke, truth meant "so joining, or separating these Representatives, as the Things they stand for, do, in themselves, agree or disagree," whereas falsity lay in "that tacit mental Proposition, wherein a conformity and resemblance is attributed to [the idea], which it has not."[20] Though not an entirely original position—it had appeared earlier in the work of Sextus Empiricus and Cicero—this view of knowledge as a matter of a correspondence between immaterial ideas and the world itself became an epistemological staple in the modern period. Epistemology demanded that the mind have a method for determining whether the ideas it grasped faithfully corresponded with the world. Modern philosophers created all kinds of fanciful schemes for making these determinations.

Despite this shift over to the view that ideas represented the world, the main similarity between ancient and modern approaches bears repeating. While the world of objects was physical and material, the ideas that represented them and with which knowledge claims were made were mental and immaterial. Despite the fact that all sense experience had to be sought out, picked up, and interpreted by particular human bodies of various shapes and sizes, modern epistemologists believed that the stuff that ended up before the mind and upon which it operated was not of any recognizably human shape or form. In taking this position, modern epistemologists had committed themselves to an almost astonishing faith in the purity of the human perceptual process. Locke flatly denied that ideas revealed any trace of their human genesis. He believed that the perceptual process was as pure and as simple as the process of a mirror reflecting its object. "These simple ideas," Locke claimed, "when offered to the mind, the Understanding can no more refuse to have, nor alter, when they are imprinted, nor blot them out, and make new ones in itself, than a mirror can refuse, alter, or obliterate the Images or Ideas, which, the Objects set before it, do therein produce."[21] Once inside, the mind's glassy essence enabled these ideas to assume the Platonic qualities of timelessness, purity, and abstractness. This was still a transcendent and detached account of knowledge. There was nothing about the character of a knowledge claim that connected it in any way to the world that it described. No sign of a grounding in the body. No sign of a grounding in the world.

The millennia of intellectual history that contributed to this approach to knowledge might make the view seem less like a particular theory about knowledge and more like an articulation of basic common sense. The theories are so deeply ingrained that it might seem like knowing could not be explained in any other way. It is sometimes hard to imagine what a possible change to this picture would look like. How could ideas not be entities that stand in front of the mind? Why would we doubt that ideas are timeless and immaterial? What else could a true belief consist in but an accurate representation of states of affairs in the world? Sometimes it takes a sustained philosophical criticism to make it clear that a view that seems like common sense is in fact a flawed theory about the nature of things. This was one of those occasions. Not long after the modern philosophers had incorporated these broadly Platonic commitments into their views of thought and belief, an old epistemological worry came back to haunt them. It was an ancient worry that suddenly appeared to be particularly urgent. The worry was skepticism.

Skepticism and the Unattached Mind

Skepticism emerged early as a problem for epistemology. It made perhaps its first appearances in the fragments of Protagoras and Heracleitus. It surfaced again in various of Socrates' debating partners and continued to appear throughout the Academic and Pyrrhonian Schools. It was discussed in the early medieval period by Augustine and later became a source of debate between Luther and Erasmus. Placed at the center of philosophical inquiry in the early modern period by Descartes, articulated in one of its most powerful forms shortly thereafter by David Hume, and then living on into the twentieth century in the form of the problem of induction, skepticism has just refused to leave philosophy alone.

To understand why the problem of skepticism has had such staying power it is necessary only to see just how easy it is to become a skeptic. Skepticism begins with the possibility of doubt. Doubt is the perennial haunt that lies behind every knowledge claim. How can we be certain that what we think is the case really *is* the case? Such doubt demands nothing more innocuous than the confession that you once held a belief that turned out to be false. But this slender crack is one through which the full force of skeptical worry can slither. As soon as people grant that some of their previous beliefs have turned out to be false, then they are compelled to admit that it is also possible for certain of their current beliefs to likewise be mistaken. In fact, there is no telling just how many current beliefs might turn out to be false. Given the ease with which skepticism can begin to eat away at a belief system, saying something about how to deal with it assumes priority status for many philosophers. Descartes offers a paradigm case of this. He began his *Meditations* by remarking: "Some years ago I was struck by the large number of falsehoods that I had accepted as true in my childhood and by the highly doubtful nature of the whole edifice that I had subsequently based on them. I realized that it was necessary once in the course of my life to demolish everything completely and start again right from the foundation if I wanted to establish anything at all in the sciences that was stable and likely to last."[22] This statement by the very first philosopher of the modern period put the defeat of skepticism at the very center of the modern discipline.

It is no coincidence that in over two thousand years of skepticism, it took on its harshest form in the modern period. At the beginning of the eighteenth century, the Scottish philosopher David Hume offered what has remained one of skepticism's most powerful statements. Adopting a conception of ideas similar to the one that both Descartes and Locke had employed, Hume noted how "the mind has never anything present to it but perceptions and cannot possibly reach any experience of their connection with objects. The supposition of such a connection . . . is, therefore, without any foundation in reasoning."[23] There is no way to make rational connections, in other words, between the ideas in front of the mind and the objects in the world outside that these ideas are supposed to be about. In fact, as both Hume and Bishop Berkeley recognized, there is no way for the moderns to rationally determine that any objects in the outside world even exist. The only things that the mind knows directly are the ideas. Judgments about the correspondence of these ideas with objects in the world are necessarily uncertain. To see just how deep this problem is, one has only to look at how desperate were both Descartes's and Locke's efforts to overcome it. Descartes relied on the benevolence of God to ensure that ideas present to his mind corresponded to the objects in the world. Locke simply asserted that no serious person could be so skeptical as to doubt the existence of the objects that the senses seem to reveal to us. Both of them chose to ignore rather than meet the challenge laid down by the skeptic. The fact that both of their attempts require a considerable amount of blind faith to succeed illustrates just how unresolvable skepticism had become in that intellectual period.

Some spent their whole lives trying to defeat the skepticism that threatened modern philosophy. Others were more sanguine. Hume himself was relatively resigned to the impossibility of defeating skepticism and calmly suggested that people should just ignore it when dealing with the practical matters of how to live everyday life. "Whatever may be the reader's opinion at this present moment," he stated, "an hour hence he will be persuaded that there is both an internal and an external world."[24] Hume would take himself off to the backgammon board whenever the profound implications of skepticism threatened to overwhelm him. There he found that he could leave behind all his doubts about the external world. But as a true philosopher, Hume must have been dismayed that only languishing in "carelessness and inattention" could rescue him from the otherwise debilitating skeptical predicament. He offered as a philosophical solution the suggestion that the mind possessed a series of coping mechanisms enabling it to fill in when necessary for its lack of ability to rationally defeat the skeptic. So, for example, custom and habit stepped in and enabled the mind to interpret two events appearing repeatedly in close succession as events that existed in a causal relationship even if direct knowledge of the causal relationship itself was always elusive. But this strategy reflected his realization that the best that the modern account could hope for was to *cope* with skepticism rather than *defeat* it.

If a mind as great as Hume's was stumped by skepticism, it is important to ask why skepticism had suddenly become so particularly devastating in the modern period. It helps to first back up a bit and try to approach the problem without the technical language. It appears to be intuitively correct that something in the very phenomenology of thinking makes skepticism unavoidable. It certainly feels as if there is an inside in which we do our thinking, our desiring, and our believing and an outside that a lot of this thinking, desiring, and believing is about. This division between inside and outside had become particularly sharp after Descartes's separation of the world into two kinds of substance, the mental and the physical. The problem was that the only things to which the mind had direct access were the ideas, and those were stuck on the inside. It was as if the skull now provided not just a physical boundary of bone and fiber between mind and world but also an epistemological boundary. The place where knowing went on had been effectively isolated from the world that its knowing was supposed to be about.

Though Descartes made the problem particularly acute, it would not be correct to lay all the blame for modern skepticism's power at his feet. Descartes had inherited a model of knowledge as something abstract, disembodied, and eternal, located in the glassy essence of the mind. He just set on top of this model his two-substance view. The ancient insistence on knowledge as something disembodied, immaterial, and universal was the start of the problem. The hyper-purity demanded of ideas began the alienation of knowledge from anything physical. Once the "forms" of the ancients had become the "ideas" of the moderns premised upon the two-substance view, the problem of hyper-purity was compounded by the need for correspondence. The nonmaterial ideas were now imprisoned inside the body with no sure way of connecting them back up to what lay outside. The problem of skepticism for the moderns was much more acute than it was for the ancients because of the radical alienation of the mental ideas from the physical world.[25] Ancient forms existed first outside of the mind and then entered the mind through the perceptual operations of the soul. Modern ideas existed *only* in the mind, with the epistemologist required to figure out how to guarantee that these ideas corresponded faithfully with what lay on the outside. Unlike the ancients, the modern mind looked upon ideas that were doubly alienated from the world. Not only were they alienated by being immaterial and universal, they were also alienated by existing only on the inside of the skull. To overcome skepticism, the modern mind would have had to successfully overcome this double alienation. This was an enormous task for something so glassy buried so deeply inside of us.

Yet despite the enormity of the task, the Cartesian picture still demanded absolute certainty of knowledge about the material world. Those demands ensured that skepticism was absolutely debilitating for the moderns. Bruno Latour has noted how the Platonic and modern pictures combined to create almost absurd demands on the modern mind. "Absolute certainty," Latour begins, "is the sort of neurotic fantasy that only a surgically removed mind would look for after it had lost everything else. . . . [O]nly a mind put in the strangest position, looking at a world *from the inside out* and linked to the outside by nothing but the tenuous connection of the *gaze,* will throb in the constant fear of losing reality; only such a bodiless observer will desperately look for some absolute life-supporting survival kit."[26] Over a period of two thousand years, epistemology had created for itself an impossible chasm between knowledge on the one hand and the world that knowledge was about on the other. Descartes had hoped that God's benevolence would guarantee the construction of a safe bridge across that chasm. But without this benevolent God, epistemologists had to struggle to construct their own bridge. With the mind characterized as an intangible glassy essence and the world made up of objects so brutally material, this was a construction project for which there were no known techniques. Epistemology had become well and truly stuck.

Two responses to this dire predicament are particularly interesting for the story I am telling. The first response, though ultimately flawed in many ways, represented a monumental attempt to do something insightful and different in the face of modern epistemology's problems. Even through its failure, this attempt illumined a creative direction in which to head. The second attempt, made nearly two centuries later, headed off in a broadly similar direction. Though still evolving, it is already clear that this second attempt has forever changed the way we look at the relation between knowledge and the world. Particularly tantalizing about this second attempt is how it sets epistemology back onto a suggestive path for environmentalists. It is this path that holds the greatest promise for those, like Shepard, who suspect that physical environments are intimately connected with thought and belief.

REATTACHING MIND AND WORLD (TAKE 1)

Although countless hours of labor had been invested between Plato and Hume in successfully increasing the storehouse of human knowledge, it was still generally believed that these intellectual achievements were achievements precisely because they carefully employed methods that enabled the rational mind to transcend the human condition and reach universal truth. As Latour correctly observed, this kind of transcendence required observers whose minds had first been surgically removed from their bodies and then bodies that had themselves been surgically removed from their emplacement in the world. Human, embodied idiosyncrasies were still believed to be nothing but an impediment to truth. To understand human knowing, one still did not need to understand anything at all about the human knower. The Christian religious context that dominated the modern period was quite content to rest with the notion that truth had a purity to it that lifted it away from the human realm. Christian philosophers shared the ancient belief that knowledge was a tap into something divine. The result, as we have seen, was a vicious skepticism made inevitable by the fact that the knower and things known had been so dramatically separated from each other. This picture remained in place until Immanuel Kant saw that the defeat of skepticism required a challenge to this separation.

Kant's dramatic rethinking of epistemology in the eighteenth century occurred in direct response to Hume. Kant was deeply impressed by the physics and mechanics that had recently been articulated by Isaac Newton. He quickly realized that Hume's skepticism undermined almost all that Newton had said. Alarmed by this possibility and unhappy with Hume's suggestion that the best the mind could do was to develop coping mechanisms for skepticism rather than to solve it, Kant woke with a start from what he called his "dogmatic slumbers." He resolved to find a way to show what Hume had denied, namely that it was possible to have universal and certain knowledge about the physical world. But since mind and world appeared to be epistemically severed from each other, where was he to start?

Kant started by considering why modern epistemology seemed to ensure that certainty would remain elusive. He saw that the supposed gap between what was in the mind and what was in the world was a good part of the problem. For the moderns, the mind had access only to what was presented in front of its inner eye. Whatever lay beyond it outside of the skin was epistemically unavailable. The judgments made about ideas could be completely and utterly wrong, and the agent of knowledge would never know it. Kant reasoned that skepticism could be defeated only if there were a way to cut through the chasm that stood between what the mind saw on the inside and what the world presented on the outside. What was in the mind and what was in the world had to be able to somehow come into contact with each other.

The way that Kant solved the problem was with a creative suggestion about what "coming into contact" could mean. Kant made the novel proposal that one of the conditions of the possibility of experience was that the shape of the world we experience was always already related to the shape of the mind. Judgments made about things picked up through the senses were not free to take any possible form. Unlike Locke, Kant did not think that the mind passively and obediently received ideas as a mirror received images. The mind had a much more active role to play in experience. The things appearing in front of the mind could not take any form whatsoever; they had to conform to certain constraints set down by the understanding mind. They had to be structured in ways that made them "sense-able" given the kind of minds we have.

To determine precisely the kind of constraining role the mind played, Kant turned to aesthetic and logical considerations. In what he tortuously called his "metaphysical deduction of the categories of the understanding," Kant attempted to show that Aristotelian logic determined a number of categories that the mind brought to experience. These categories included substance, cause, unity, and negation. The categories supplied a necessary structure for judgments about the physical world. Without the imposition of the categories, there could be no coherence to experience at all. But there was an important corollary to the metaphysical deduction of the categories. The world itself could not be put under those categories unless there was something about its appearance that made it compatible with them. In his "transcendental deduction of the categories" Kant showed that the world indeed must appear that way. Without that appearance, the world would not be something that could be coherently experienced. At the end of these arguments, the two deductions satisfied Kant that some truths—for example, truths about causation and about substance—could be known with certainty about the world. This certainty was assured because, for knowledge to be possible at all, world and mind had to be capable of fitting together in a process that Kant called a "transcendental synthesis." What came in through the senses was immediately synthesized with the categories imposed by the mind. Meaningful experience was possible only because this synthesis could occur. Kant realized that in making these suggestions about experience, he had turned on its head almost everything that had come before it in epistemology. By suggesting that the world had to appear a certain way because of the existence of pregiven mental structures, Kant for the first time gave the mind an active role in determining the content of knowledge. The physical world did not call all the shots in determining how worldly objects appeared to observers. The mind called some shots of its own. Kant called this complete change of perspective his "Copernican Revolution" in epistemology.

The full details of how Kant made this case in *The Critique of Pure Reason* remains one of the most complex sustained arguments in philosophy. We go no further into it here. The important lesson to draw is about what had to happen in the face of modern skepticism. The capacities of the mind had to be taken into account when explaining why we experience what we do. The mistake made by modern empiricist epistemology up to that point had been to suppose that the mind was completely uninvolved in experience, receiving impressions as a mirror receives images. A. C. Ewing described Kant's innovation as that of recognizing that "we are neither wholly active nor wholly passive in knowledge. We do not create what we know, yet we do not accept the evidence concerning other things passively from our senses but tamper with it."[27] With the mind adopting this active role, the problem of how to get the ideas in the mind to reflect or represent the structure of the world is neatly sidestepped. Knowledge no longer requires hoping that immaterial ideas perfectly represent the physical world. There is no longer an epistemic chasm between mind and world. Knowledge has become a product of an artful interaction between the knower and the things that the knower experiences. The alienation inherited through two millennia of epistemology between what was in the mind and what was in the world had been broken.

Kant's proposal bears enormous significance for the story I am telling. Caught in the grip of a Platonic approach to knowledge that insisted on an absolute separation of mind and world, Kant's predecessors included no details about the human doing the knowing in their accounts of how knowledge gets constructed. Neither Locke nor Descartes ever suspected that facts about the human mind could be connected to the shape of what appeared in front of the mind. Kant's radical approach countered skepticism not by finding a way to cross the chasm between objects outside in the world and ideas inside the skull but by never letting the chasm open up in the first place. Kant insisted that both world and mind are always simultaneously contributing something to the shape of knowledge. The mind sets some conditions that the world is forced to meet if it is to be experienced. The world, fortunately, can meet them. Knowledge then becomes a synthesis of something brought by the world and something brought by the mind of the person making the knowledge claim. In Kant's synthesis, skepticism is avoided because mind and world are never epistemologically alienated from each other in the first place.

Kant's position, while certainly ingenious, had certain flaws. German idealists liked the fact that the way the world appeared was controlled by laws that were brought to experience by the knowing agent. If you were not careful, the important role of the physical world in the synthesis Kant had described could be neglected. Knowledge could then start to look like something wholly created by the human agent. Idealists extended Kant's position in this direction and, in the process, managed to call into question the significance of the physical world. A second major flaw lay in the limited lens through which Kant was prepared to view the connections between mind and world. On Kant's account, everything that the human agent brought to the epistemological table was in the form of logical structure. This meant that the synthesis necessary for knowledge involved humans only in so far as they were a vehicle for bringing these logical necessities to bear. Kant had finally made certain details about human knowers relevant to our understanding of truth and knowledge, but these details regrettably remained rather abstract and detached. The human as a concrete, flesh-and-blood, embodied being still eluded epistemology. Knowledge had been reattached to *some* of the details of the human knower, but it had not been reattached to the right kind of details. Latour's neurotic, surgically removed mind had been brought back into *some* contact with the world but not quite the right kind of contact. A good deal of the alienation between mind and world remained in place. As a result, Kant's efforts did not succeed in the way that they might have done. Nor did they provide quite the right kind of platform from which to reattach place and mind. But as is usually the case with good ideas, Kant's synthesis refused to go away. In 1969, the basic insight was resurrected in a slightly different but, we shall see, much improved form. This occurred in a remarkably similar situation to the one faced by Kant. The question once again was about what to do to defeat Humean skepticism.

REATTACHING MIND AND WORLD (TAKE 2)

In the mid–twentieth century, an American analytic philosopher named Willard Van Orman Quine spent a considerable amount of time ruminating on just how intractable the problem of skepticism had been for modern epistemology. Looking carefully at what had happened in the most recent failed attempt to give knowledge some reliable foundations, Quine began to plot his way around the problem. His solution proceeded along lines that bear more than a skin-deep resemblance to those employed by Kant.

At the time Quine was writing, the latest attempt to overcome skepticism about knowledge claims, pursued with considerable zeal by a group known as the logical positivists, had for some time been foundering on some fairly familiar shoals. The logical positivists described themselves as the intellectual heirs of Hume, so it is little surprise to find them running up against some of the same problems. Logical positivists began with the desire to have their account of knowledge be as simple and as scientific as possible. To ensure this, they determined that there could be only two components of every meaningful knowledge claim, propositions about states of affairs in the world and universal laws of logic. The propositions were themselves held to a fairly strict standard. Following Wittgenstein's lead in his *Tractatus,* logical positivists applied the verifiability principle of meaning to their propositions. This principle held that the full extent of the meaning of a proposition was nothing but the method of its empirical verification. Logical positivists insisted that those propositions that could not be empirically verified, such as metaphysical and ethical claims, were meaningless.

Things started to come apart when logical positivists tried to be precise about how to effectively work with the verifiability principle of meaning. One immediate and mildly irritating problem that could have stopped them in their tracks was that the verifiability principle itself was not actually verifiable.

There was no way to verify with experience the truth of the principle that the meaning of a proposition is nothing but the method of verifying it. By its own standard, then, the verifiability principle was meaningless. Wittgenstein suggested that the only way to solve this problem was to read and understand the implication of the verifiability principle of meaning and then discard it, no longer regarding it as part of one's stock of knowledge about the world.

Unfortunately, even with this little problem set aside, there were plenty of other more troubling puzzles ahead. The most significant ones arose over the question of how the verification of a proposition might actually occur. Experience was supposed to be able to verify whether a proposition really represented a fact. But it was unclear exactly how it would do this. A state of affairs in the world is a different kind of thing from a proposition, and an experience is, in turn, different from both of these. Propositions were supposed to somehow represent states of affairs in the world. But it was unclear exactly what form this representation would take. Given this uncertainty, the critics of positivism wondered exactly how positivists might verify that the proposition doing the representing did in fact represent the state of affairs in the world. It could not be that the proposition was verified by virtue of its being an accurate report on an entirely subjective experience because that would have been far too private a basis for the foundation of all knowledge. There would have been no guarantee that what one person took to be a verification would be viewed that way by another. And even without this problem of the private nature of experience there remained the more general problem of explaining how a proposition could capture the full richness of what lay in a subjective experience.

Logical positivists faced numerous other difficulties when they tried to reconstruct empirical science out of verifiable propositions and logic. But the basic problem of how to verify a proposition is the one of most interest because of how closely it resembles the problem faced by the moderns of how to be sure that an idea placed in front of the mind's eye corresponded with the world. The problem had changed its form slightly. Philosophy had for the most part moved away from modern notions of ghostly mental entities populating machinelike bodies. Epistemology was no longer about the ideas presented to the inner eye of these ghosts. The propositions of the logical positivists were things that could in principle exist out in the world, written down and analyzed with linguistic and philosophical tools. However, in terms of how the epistemologist was going to connect those propositions securely with the world, logical positivists seemed to be in no better a position than the moderns. Though the problem was no longer exclusively based on the presence of an inside/outside split, it was still the problem of how to be sure that the immaterial thing that carried knowledge—in this case the proposition—accurately represented things in the material world.

The proponents of logical positivism were not unaware of the difficulties, and they expended a considerable amount of energy trying to resolve them. Rudolf Carnap, Otto Neurath, Morris Schlick, and Ernest Mach each suggested ways of interpreting the relationship between experience and propositions that would accommodate some of the puzzles that had been raised about verification. But it seemed that no revision could guarantee a secure link between the proposition and the world that it concerned. Even Morris Schlick, as eager as anyone to see logical positivism succeed in one form or another, admitted that "as soon as one asks about the certainty with which one may maintain the truth of [protocol] propositions . . . one has to admit that it is exposed to all manner of doubt."[28] Perhaps the best that propositions could do, some logical positivists argued, was to agree with other propositions. But if this was the case, then where had the world gone to in this compromise?

When Quine looked at logical positivism's failure and considered this failure in the light of the history of epistemology, he saw a familiar pattern repeating itself. This pattern took the form of increasingly desperate attempts to save the incorrigibility of knowledge claims derived from sense experience. The problem began as soon as a unit such as an idea or a proposition was selected to be the building block out of which to construct accounts of the world. Try as they might, epistemologists had been unable to guarantee the accuracy of any representation due to a gap between the units intended to bear the weight of the representation and the state of affairs in the world that the finished representation was supposed to mirror. The unit carrying the representation was always too alienated from the world to be sure of faithfully representing it. Quine noted with some resignation, "I do not see that we are farther along today than where Hume left us."[29]

Despite the fact that Hume had ably pointed out the intractability of the problem associated with this way of approaching epistemology and that Kant had gone to enormous lengths to indicate a direction for circumventing it, logical positivists had become stuck in almost exactly the same place as had Locke and Descartes. Rather than look at this as a call to renew efforts to defeat skepticism, Quine saw it as a lesson to accept it. "The Humean predicament," he quipped, "is the human predicament."[30] He recognized that some of the logical positivists, most notably Carnap and Neurath, might have already seen through their struggles that the quest for Cartesian certainty was a lost cause. But only Quine saw the opportunity that this presented to do something different.

Like Kant, Quine was a lateral thinker. He decided that skepticism demanded nothing less than changing the goals of epistemology. In so doing he opened up some interesting epistemological avenues. Instead of starting over and attempting to determine how to finally ensure that statements about the world could be proven to correspond exactly with how the world in fact is, Quine accepted the hand that humans had been dealt. Epistemologists would always fail in their attempts to ensure certainty in belief if certainty meant being sure that some immaterial knowledge-bearing entity corresponded exactly with something in the world. This was not, according to Quine, a cause for despair, but rather was a call to focus epistemological inquiry on something else. An equally interesting task, thought Quine, would be to investigate empirically the question of how beliefs do in fact get formed. The fact that humans are able to use experience to create such elaborate and complex theories to describe the world needs some explaining. Epistemology, Quine thought, might better try to explain how it is that humans manage to move miraculously from "two-dimensional optical projections . . . various impacts of airwaves on ear drums, some gaseous reactions in the nasal passages and a few kindred odds and ends" to, say, the theory of relativity.[31] Most importantly, these were questions that could be answered through the natural sciences. Quine shared with Locke, Hume, and the logical positivists the view that all knowledge originates in the stimulation of sense receptors. His insight was to see that epistemology should concern itself with explaining scientifically what happens in theory production after these receptors are stimulated.

Scientifically investigating belief formation meant "naturalizing epistemology" by drawing on the best current theories in the sciences to account for how humans form beliefs. It meant using the descriptive power of the sciences to give epistemology a hand. Implicitly recognized by all naturalized epistemologies is the basic but significant Darwinian insight that the place of humanity is firmly in the natural order. When human agents attempt to construct knowledge, they are acting as part of the physical and biological world and obeying all the relevant natural laws. With epistemology naturalized, knowing is no different in kind from other natural activities such as breathing, talking, or digesting. A science that investigates how we know should accordingly proceed not much differently from a science that investigates how we digest. Quine suggested that if you take this tack, then epistemology "simply falls into place as a chapter of psychology. It studies a natural phenomenon, viz., a physical human subject."[32] When Quine made this call in 1969, empirical psychology was not a very developed science, so there was little immediate progress made in answering the empirical questions. However, what is significant in terms of the direction of this move is how, for the second time in the history of epistemology, a proposed reorientation in response to Humean skepticism prompted a fundamental break from the Platonic legacy. And Quine's reorientation was considerably more dramatic than Kant's.

Though separated by about two hundred years, both Quine and Kant saw that the inherited alienation of mind and world created an unsolvable skeptical problem. Both of them responded to this skepticism by recognizing that epistemology needed to explain the role that the person doing the knowing played in creating the knowledge claim. Both denied the Lockean assumption that the knower was passive and irrelevant to the shape of ideas. Both men, in effect, addressed the problematic gap between the world and the knowledge claim by insisting that the person making the knowledge claim made an active and interesting contribution to its shape. Kant and Quine replaced the passive mind of the moderns with an active and engaged mind that made an important contribution to the shape of a belief.

Though the form of Quine's response to skepticism was broadly similar to Kant's, the details were different in significant ways. Although both began by recognizing that the agent of knowledge influences what can be known, Kant determined these influences by looking transcendentally at what logic demands of a rational judgment. Quine, on the other hand, looked for his influences through an empirical investigation of an agent's cognitive system. Whereas Kant involved the logical mind, Quine involved the biological brain. Quine let go of some weighty epistemological baggage by recognizing the fact that humans are natural creatures who operate according to biological laws. Kant's arguments were based on a Christian, creationist perspective in which reason and logic were still the keys to separating humans from the rest of nature. Quine, with the benefit of Darwin, studied human knowing scientifically just as he would have studied any other kind of organismic activity in nature.

Also gone from the Platonic inheritance was the idea that knowledge claims have to be universal and true for all time. Theories about the world were, for Quine, pragmatic devices. Beliefs were required to cohere with a web made up of all the other beliefs that a person held. In Quine's view, beliefs did not get evaluated one at a time but met the tribunal of sense experience as a whole system. Whether a set of experiences refuted or confirmed a particular belief depended on the adjustments that people were prepared to make to other beliefs in their system. With coherence as the goal, theories and beliefs did not have to meet the strict standard of absolute certainty. Irrefutability was unreasonable. No longer cut off from the physical world about which they were theorizing, those claiming knowledge had been released from that particular neurotic fantasy. Being *in* the world rather than detached from it invited a more pragmatic orientation.

It is certainly the case that Kant's revision of epistemology was more challenging than Quine's. Kant wanted to defeat skepticism whereas Quine sought only to change the topic. Perhaps it might be legitimately objected that all Quine had done in response to skepticism was to choose an easier set of questions, questions he thought epistemologists might be better equipped to successfully answer. But there is another way to interpret his pragmatic move toward a naturalized epistemology that fits better with the goal of bringing accounts of knowledge back in touch with the earth. That is to say that Quine had recognized how Cartesians, Lockeans, logical positivists, and hundreds of others like them had fallen prey to the fantasies that haunt a surgically removed mind. The way to eliminate those harmful fantasies was to begin to reattach the mind to the very things that it was supposed to know. To reduce the alienation of the mind, it was necessary to begin to give the mind back its earthly context. As Latour put it, this is the project of "plugging the wriggling and squiggling brain back into its withering body." [33] Putting the knowing mind back in this context would lower the stakes for a disembodied mind that had become lost to the world it was supposed to describe.

Thanks to Quine, epistemology had for the first time pulled itself out of the armchair and rejected the rather sedentary introspective activity it had traditionally employed as its method. Quine's call to pursue epistemology through empirical psychology ensured that people and not just their beliefs should be the objects of scientific study. "Better to discover how [knowledge] is in fact developed and learned than to fabricate a fictitious structure to similar effect," he suggested. [34] Gone was the belief that knowing is a matter of transcending one's physical situation in order to know the world, Godlike, from nowhere. Important facts about the cognitive makeup of the knower became relevant to the question of how it is that the knower comes to know. Quine, like Kant, asked that knowledge be looked upon as the product of a cooperative relationship between empirical content supplied by the world and the particular shape of the human brain.

Once an epistemologist rejects the part of the tradition that holds that the nature of the knower is irrelevant to what he or she can know, the person making a knowledge claim changes from being just a passive recorder of information into being an active and interesting participant in the knowledge process. Paying attention to the physical nature and situation of the knowledge maker yields an epistemology that is newly engaged with the world. In this project, epistemological argument no longer need be transcendental. Knowing is no longer treated as the formulaic activity of disembodied rational selves. It is the story of wriggling and squiggling brains transforming sensory stimulations into fallible knowledge claims. And even though Quine did not appreciate it at the time, the wiggling, squiggling brain belongs in a wriggling, squiggling body that itself moves through a living, breathing, multidimensional world replete with texture and color. This is potentially rich and rewarding epistemic territory to explore. It prescribes an inherently grounded investigation demanding that epistemologists consider the real-world conditions of knowledge production. These real-world conditions involve bodies and cultures that do their knowing immersed in the fascinating details of multiple and heterogeneous physical environments. In this we can begin to see the first glimmer of what Shepard had called the "strange but necessary connection between place and mind." It is also the beginning of the grounding of knowledge.

We pass through a stand of the rarest of things;
old-growth, high-altitude lodgepole that survived
the fire. These trees have the genetics we need:
they've survived beyond their years, avoided bug
infestations, evaded the infamous fire of 1910, as
well as this most recent 1994 fire. They've lived up
here at the top of the world, immersed to the hilt
in the glories of natural selection, and now we're
going to erase all that work, all that grace,
all that meaning.

Rick Bass, *The Book of the Yaak*

2   Grounding Knowledge

The study of mind, thought, and belief simply had to
change after Quine. Holding out for a disconnected mind constructing knowledge claims in isolation from any kind of facts about the thinker's physical situation would have meant moving back down the same old path toward skepticism. Kant and Quine both saw how the intractability of skepticism was the product of a view of knowledge as disconnected from any of the details about the knower and his or her world. Both determined that the knower had to be *involved* in some way in knowledge production rather than being just the passive recipient of images reflected from nature. So they each reconnected thought to the world by allowing humans to bring some their own structure to experience. Kant suggested structure in the form of categories determined by logic. Quine added Darwinian insights and brought in features of the biological brain as relevant influences on knowledge. Both recognized that world and mind are together involved in every thought. Once Quine had naturalized the insight, something importantly ecological became clear. Thought does not lift us clear of anything. It is a form of contextualized expression that emerges directly out of our earthly situation.

Whereas both of these thinkers provided a helpful direction away from skepticism and the old view of mind as a glassy essence, neither of them said much about places being relevant to the study of knowledge.[1] Mind or brain was the extent of the worldly involvement that either could manage in their epistemologies. But as this chapter discusses, the common insight opens an important door. It is a door that can lead us directly outside and into the richness of the natural world. Once the knowledge maker is involved at even the minimal level articulated by Kant and Quine, the physical environment cannot fail to sneak its way into epistemology.

Since Quine made his breakthrough, epistemologists have tended to offer one of two different kinds of explanations for how the knower's worldly situation is relevant to knowledge. At the risk of oversimplification, these approaches can be called the "scientific" and the "cultural" approaches to naturalizing.[2] The former is more traditionally Quinean because it pursues a scientific investigation of the biological and physiological factors that shape knowledge. The latter departs somewhat from Quine's intentions and focuses on cultural factors. But both are products of the turn toward participating, grounded agents of knowledge that the problem of skepticism demanded. And both approaches ultimately point in a suggestive direction for the environmentalist. After thirty years of looking carefully at what the worldly situation of the knower contributes, something important has begun to emerge. Once the details of the person making the knowledge claim are put under scrutiny, epistemologists have found themselves increasingly having to look back out from the person toward the constitutive relationships the person has with the world around him or her. Epistemologists have found that just as one cannot tell the whole story about knowing minds by isolating them from any connection to their brains, so one cannot tell the whole story about knowing brains by isolating them from any connection to the bodies and the environments in which they operate. Knowledge claims emerge from wider contexts than just the mind or the biological brain. This apparent need to look at the wider contexts in which knowledge gets made might helpfully be called the need to *richly situate knowledge*. It is these wider contexts that take us outside and into the physical environment.

Paths from Scientific Naturalizing to Environment

The first approach to situating the knower, the one that Quine thought was the only approach, involves using the natural sciences to determine how the biological brain allows the human organism to construct beliefs about the world. This approach quickly takes us away from our original concern with epistemology and into the realm of cognitive science. Since scientific studies of mind are not often considered to be in the province of traditional philosophical research, philosophers have often tended to be rather ambivalent about this approach.[3] Adding to this ambivalence, scientific studies of mind have until recently been completely inadequate to the task that Quine had set for them. Philosophers did not really miss anything if they failed to pay attention to the stories being told in cognitive science. As a result, epistemologists have been slow to fully bite Quine's bullet and to scientifically naturalize their accounts of human knowing.

But such ambivalence is becoming less and less defensible. Both ancient Greek and modern epistemology reflected particular views about what the mind is and how it relates to the body. These views were based on contemporary empirical evidence, even if that evidence was not very sophisticated at the time. Scientific studies of mind now reveal considerably more about how it is that humans go about constructing their beliefs. The time during which the ambivalence of epistemologists to cognitive science was acceptable is fast running out. Epistemologists who take Darwin seriously must be willing to follow Quine at least some of the way down the scientific naturalizing path. Given that all other events in nature are studied using the natural sciences, Darwinians should be reluctant to exempt certain activities of the human animal from that kind of study. No epistemologist should accept an account of knowing incompatible with what the natural sciences reveal about the way that the human organism actually operates in the world.

Two main approaches to scientific naturalizing with cognitive science stand out. The first is discussed briefly, just enough to illustrate why it cannot be considered a promising approach. The second approach is discussed in considerably more depth because of the way that it appears to incorporate some of the epistemological insights Kant and Quine demanded. This second way of looking at cognition supplies the most fertile ground for the claims to be made in subsequent chapters.

The invention of digital computers made possible what was initially the most promising strain of cognitive science. Varela, Thompson, and Rosch labeled this strain the "cognitivist" approach to the study of mind in their helpful typology.[4] The approach is characterized by the belief that the human cognitive processing system is the type of system that can be accurately modeled on digital computers. Cognitivism employs the metaphor of intelligence as linear computation. The computerlike mind receives discrete inputs that it first codifies into symbols and then processes according to formal rules in order to produce discrete outputs. The brain works as a complicated symbol manipulator. The neurobiology of the brain functionally resembles the electronic circuitry found in a computer.

The cognitivist approach seems to be intuitively plausible, but its disadvantages soon become apparent. One difficult problem centers on the question of how to explain the connection between the proposed computational processes and the conscious experience of thought. The subjective experience of thought becomes, at best, a strange and accidental by-product of computational processes, a mere epiphenomenon. Subjective experience is just tacked on top of the more interesting neurocircuitry. Making the subjective feeling of consciousness only an epiphenomenon presents cognitivists with what is sometimes referred to as the "mind-mind problem." This is the problem of having to reconcile the mind as a set of biochemical processes with the mind as the seat of rich and compelling subjective experiences. Cognitivists seem to create too much distance between the computational and the phenomenal mind, leaving us wallowing in the face of a kind of philosophical schizophrenia.

A second problem with the cognitivist approach should particularly bother us, given the story told so far. Cognitivism retains the skepticism-producing gap between the units in the mind responsible for beliefs, on the one hand, and the world that the beliefs are supposed to involve, on the other. This risks reintroducing the same problem that modern and logical positivist epistemologists had failed to overcome. Cognitivist models see the brain as essentially a symbol manipulator. Between inputs and outputs the brain performs certain operations on symbols that in some way represent the world. The question of whether the symbols do in fact faithfully represent the world remains just as sharp as ever. The cognitivist account is, to be sure, an account much more scientifically informed than the accounts offered in the modern period. Ideas presented on an internal screen to the mind have been replaced by symbols manipulated in the brain's neurocircuitry. But like the ideas of the moderns, the symbols are still expected to represent the world in certain ways, and they are still nonmaterial entities that effectively disconnect thought entirely from the stuff of the world that the thought concerns. This picture retains several of the problematic Platonic themes even if they are dressed in more contemporary garb. Given just how deep the Platonic assumptions run in traditional views of thought, it is not surprising that early approaches to cognitive science unwittingly reinscribed some of them. But because we have come to naturalizing epistemology as a way to escape the problem of skepticism, it seems prudent to avoid opting for a naturalized account of cognition that risks running back into the same difficulties.

A third reason to be suspicious of the cognitivist approach is that it fails to view cognition as being involved in any way with the particularities of bodies. Thought is still something that goes on in the spaces between the inputs and the outputs of a complex symbol manipulator. There appears to be no need for this system to be plugged in to anything resembling an organism. Knowing is still isolated from the world, deep inside the circuitry of some cognizing machine. Cognitivism has not put thought and belief back in the wriggling, squiggling body as Latour had recommended. This isolation is worrying. Cognitivist minds, if they were to exist, seem to be alienated enough that they would still be prey to the neurotic fantasies to which Descartes and his followers had fallen victim. A symbol manipulator approach, a brain/body split, and an input/output model that completely separates cognitive processes from the world that those processes are supposed to represent looks far too much like the modern picture that has been discredited. If epistemologies are to absorb the lessons learned though Kant and Quine, then they are going to have to look somewhere else for their richly naturalized scientific account.

Varela, Thompson, and Rosch label the contemporary approach to cognition that overcomes many of these problems the "enactivist approach." Unlike cognitivism, the enactivist approach is acutely aware of the problems inherent in reinscribing Platonic and modernist credos into cognitive science. It rejects the idea of cognition as a matter of an alienated, internal mind receiving sensory information about an external world from which it is functionally isolated. It also rejects the idea that cognition is any kind of symbol manipulation process, with the symbols assumed to represent the world in some way. Instead of attempting to represent an independent world through a series of isolated internal processes, enactivist approaches to cognition follow Kant's lead and recognize that the inputs and the cognitive structures that operate on those inputs cannot be entirely separated from one another. This account of cognition insists that the world appears in a way that reflects certain facts about how cognition works. Varela, Thompson, and Rosch describe this kind of cognition as "enact[ing] a world as a domain of distinctions that is inseparable from the structure embodied by the cognitive system."[5] Enactivists therefore incorporate the important Kantian synthesis between mind and world. In so doing they take seriously the role of the human being in shaping knowledge.

A key Darwinian innovation going far beyond the one introduced by Quine lies at the heart of enactivism. Enactivists concur with Richard Rorty's recent observation that "representation, as opposed to increasingly complex adaptive behavior, is hard to integrate with an evolutionary story."[6] Enactivist accounts not only take seriously the constraints brought about by brain function, but they also endeavor to interpret those constraints in the context of a brain located *in* a head *on* a body that *moves about an environment.* In other words, they refuse to consider the activities of the brain in isolation from the walking, talking, feeding, and perceiving activities of the whole animal. They do not just situate cognition; they *richly* situate it in the context of the full range of activities that the organism performs. Sensorimotor activity in an environment is regarded as making a key contribution to thought. Varela, Thompson, and Rosch call this kind of cognition "embodied action." Their careful explanation of this term goes as follows:

> [B]y using the phrase embodied we mean to highlight two points: first, that cognition depends upon the kinds of experience that come from having a body with various sensori-motor capacities, and second, that these individual sensori-motor capacities are themselves embedded in a more encompassing biological, psychological, and cultural context. By using the term action we mean to emphasize once again that sensory and motor processes, perception and action, are fundamentally inseparable in lived cognition. Indeed, the two are not merely contingently linked in individuals; they have evolved together.[7]

So the enactivist mind is an evolved mind, one connected to both the body and to the body's various activities in the different environments in which it finds itself.

This approach has a reputable pedigree. The importance of understanding cognition as being derived from embodied activity also appeared in the work of Jean Piaget. Piaget's primary interest was in childhood development. He sought to explain the progression that a child makes from the state of relative helplessness at birth to the considerable autonomy exhibited by the time of early childhood. He speculated that the formation of certain sensorimotor patterns, which he labeled "schemas," played an important role in this process. Piaget defined a schema as "the generalizable characteristics of [an] action, that is, those which allow the repetition of the same action or its application to a new content."[8] Schemas are the structures that enable an infant to cope in the world. They take the form of embodied patterns of interaction that infants can employ in similar situations.

Schemas not only make possible sensorimotor action in the world, but they are also *products* of these interactions. A few schemas, such as those necessary for breathing, suckling, and grasping, are present at birth. The rest are learned through embodied experience. A child's repertoire of schemas changes and evolves over time, tempered by biological constraints and body-world interactions. New schemas cannot be created out of nothing. They are a product of schemas already in existence, which are added to and amended by further embodied experience in the world.

Piaget makes the move from sensorimotor action to cognition by essentially erasing the boundary between the two. He makes it into a difference of degree rather than a difference of kind. His account of childhood development includes the movement toward the increasingly formal and abstract utilization of schemas. Generalization from schemas that govern particular sensorimotor functions allows for cognitive development through four stages of maturity that Piaget termed the sensorimotor, the pre-operational, the operational, and the formal operational. By the time the individual has reached the formal operational level, he or she can engage in the kind of abstract thought that produces knowledge. At this final stage, Piaget's account can be regarded not just as a story of sensorimotor achievement but as the basis of an epistemology. Mary Hesse and Michael Arbib, in their 1986 Gifford Lectures, sketched how to turn Piaget's account of childhood development into a complete theory of knowledge. [9] They described their approach as resting on "a theory of the embodied self, rooting human knowledge in the body's interaction with the world." [10]

Even though Piaget's innovation appears to be primarily about the connection between action and thought, if you look closely you also see a familiar Kantian insight buried in such an epistemology. The world cannot, according to Piaget, present any of its own intrinsic properties to the infant. If it is to be comprehensible at all, experience must already be shaped by existing schemas, just as experience for Kant had to be already shaped by the existing categories of the understanding. Contemporary schema theorists Hesse and Arbib describe Piaget's position as a "dynamic Kantianism." The Kantianism lies in the structure that the agent of knowledge brings to all experience. The dynamism lies in the fact that for Piaget these structures are continually evolving as we interact with the world, while for Kant they were fixed transcendentally. [11]

The most complete articulation of enactivist cognitive science is found not in any disciples of Piaget but in the account of cognition developed by Mark Johnson in *The Body in the Mind*. [12] Though his work is not primarily in epistemology but in philosophical psychology, Johnson has begun to supply many of the missing pieces of a scientifically naturalized approach to knowledge that would start to do justice to the embodied nature of mind. Like Piaget and like Hesse and Arbib, Johnson employs the notion of an embodied schema. He defines a schema as "a recurring, dynamic pattern of our perceptual inter-actions and motor programs that gives coherence and structure to our ex-perience."[13] He also suggests that most of these schemas have their genesis in organism-environment interactions. It is because humans are embodied crea-tures, embedded in particular but constantly changing situations, that we need image schemas in the first place. In his collaborations with George Lakoff, Johnson has identified a number of schemas that have particular importance for the human situation. These schemas go by names such as "contact," "part-whole," "center-periphery," and "balance." Though this is not the place to re-hearse them, Johnson gives eight kinds of empirical evidence for their exis-tence. He then supplies the important details of how embodied schemas are connected to cognition.[14]

The balance schema is given the most extensive treatment in *The Body in the Mind*. The sensorimotor pattern that manages to keep us upright most of the time is the balance schema. It is clear that this schema emerges out of experiences in the world possible only for creatures with a particular type of body. The bipedal, erect nature of human posture makes balance particularly important. The location of the head with all its important organs on the top of the body some distance above the ground ensures that the failure to succeed at balance has rather deleterious effects on survival. Balance is important to the body in several different ways: for standing upright, for carrying equal loads in each hand, and in the experience of homeostasis in bodily organs. The body learns particular sensorimotor patterns that it can rely on to maintain these kinds of balance. In the different situations that require balance the body will quickly deploy these schemas. Because we live with balance all of our lives, our successful deployment of the balance schema occurs almost unnoticed most of the time. "The experience of balance," says Johnson, "is so pervasive and so absolutely basic for our coherent experience of the world, and our survival in it, that we are seldom ever aware of it" (74). We become habituated to balanc-ing to such an extent that we rarely need to exert any effort in order to stay upright. Balancing becomes a habit, and a good habit to get into.

The bodily experience of balance generates schemas that, at a sensorimo-tor level, ensure that the body becomes good at staying upright. Johnson then goes on to suggest that schemas such as the balance schema can be extended to applications beyond sensorimotor function. This is the most provocative and controversial part of the thesis. He thinks this extension is possible because schemas have "definite internal structure that can be figuratively extended to structure our understanding of formal relations among concepts and propo-sitions" (38).[15] The physical logic that embodied actors discover in the world is literally incorporated into the body via sensorimotor schemas and is later called upon to help supply structure to thought. For example, the balance schema keeps us upright, but it also provides the structure for our conception of legal justice, moral fairness, psychological health, systemic balance, and mathematical equality. The balance schema turns out to be particularly central to cognition. It is only because humans are bipedal and erect that the balance schema comes to be so important. If humans moved around like millipedes, if they had much lower centers of gravity, or if their most sensitive organs were in their feet, then the balance schema would be less important. Humans learn about balance, not by being taught it, but by feeling it with their bodies. Fish do not experience this because they cannot fall over or carry loads on each fin. If humans were marine mammals, the balance schema would likely be of less significance. The important insight here lies in the connection between thought and embodied action. The structures that help us get around our physical world are the basis of those that help us get around our cognitive world. "The locus of reason," Johnson writes with George Lakoff, turns out to be "the same as the locus of sensori-motor control." [16]

Though this account of the embodied mind is controversial, it does point us in a direction consistent with the Kantianism in Quine and the dynamism in Piaget. Cognition is not only *in* and *of* the world as Quine had wanted; it is also *in* and *of* a body that acts in the world as Piaget had insisted. With cognition connected so firmly to the particularities of our physical embodiment, then Thomas Nagel is correct in his famous insight about the impossibility of knowing what it would be like to be inside the head of another creature such as a bat. Humans could not possibly know what it is like to be a bat. The most important thing required to think like a bat is, in fact, to actually be embodied as a bat!

Most of the scientific naturalizers who have followed Quine failed, as he himself did, to realize that the body is central to a richly naturalized epistemology. In an aptly titled article, "What Is Natural about Epistemology Naturalized?" feminist epistemologist Lorraine Code points out how scientific naturalizers of epistemology typically refuse to imagine that humans are anything more than just information processors. Code offers the correction that we are actually "marvelously corporeal," embodied actors. [17] N. Katherine Hayles also weighs in on the centrality of the body to epistemology when she insists: "the particular form of our embodiment matters for it determines the nature of our interactions with the world. Far from interfering with scientific inquiry, interaction is the necessary precondition for acquiring any knowledge about the world at all." [18]

Enactivism shows much promise for being an important way into a richly situated epistemology. Unlike cognitivism, it succeeds in incorporating both the Kantian and the Quinean insights. Humans are active participants in the knowledge process, their schemas shape experience, and this influence is one that can be studied by the natural sciences. But enactivism takes us considerably beyond Quine and in doing so provides both some important guidelines and some suggestive possibilities for how we should look at thought and belief. First, it is clear that enactivism serves to connect cognition to the rest of the body of the organism and not just to its brain. Cognition is not something that can be understood by studying the mind independently of the body in which it is located. An enactivist account that pays due attention to the body, such as Johnson's, recognizes this fact and places it at the heart of cognition. A second point in its favor is that enactivism gives us an account of mind that coheres with evolutionary theory. Mind is an extension of the structures necessary for sensorimotor experience. Evolution strongly supports this view. It is a view that closes the gap between thinking and nonthinking organisms. Thought becomes less of a quasi-divine capacity and more of an animal activity. This view is fully consistent with the fact that thought evolved out of the activities of animals that moved, ate, slept, got into fights, and successfully manipulated their environments even before they engaged in activities similar to the ones that we are prepared to call "thought." Third, and perhaps most significant for current purposes, enactivism potentially connects the activities of the mind with the details of the physical environment. As soon as it has been granted that the whole body is crucial to our understanding of cognition, it becomes clear that it is a mistake to consider that body in isolation as a kind of body-in-a-vat. Bodily activity takes place in an ambient environment. Because of this, enactivism opens up the intriguing possibility that differences between the sensorimotor, embodied activities of individuals in different environments might have some relevance for cognition. It provides a reason for tempering the idea that thought has a single universal and fixed structure independent of all physical context.[19]

Johnson appears almost ready to recognize this third point in his account. It is not just the body but the kind of things that this body does in its world that gives the shape to cognitive structures. His image schematic approach describes "structures that emerge from our experience as bodily organisms functioning in interaction with an environment."[20] We develop the balance schema through embodied action in a physical world that has a particular character. If thought is intimately linked with sensorimotor processes, and if these processes vary to any significant extent from environment to environment, then we might expect that different environments will offer different resources for thought. We saw that living in a terrestrial environment makes balance more important than it would be in a marine environment. This is a hint of an emerging link between place and mind. With the thinking process brought so solidly back down to earth, the Platonic and modernist inheritance has been left far behind, and the grounding of knowledge has truly begun.

I suggested earlier that a richly naturalized epistemology is a complex and exciting territory to explore. Things have already been made interesting by adding first the body and then the physical environment to the discussion of how best to understand the shape of thought and belief. But this does not exhaust the possibilities. Individuals do not exist just in physical environments; they also exist in complex social and cultural environments that lend distinctive shape to what those individuals say, think, and believe. This suggests the need for another type of situating to address how beliefs are informed by social and cultural environments. Those that have pursued this other main type of naturalizing—"cultural naturalizing"—address this task.

Paths from Cultural Naturalizing to Environment

Rather than approaching knowledge by considering a natural scientist's account of how the mind functions as Quine had intended, another group of epistemologists turned instead to historical, ethnographic, and sociological methods to determine how theory building occurs. These theorists are the cultural naturalizers. Some epistemologists might immediately object that the term "cultural naturalizing" appears oxymoronic. Naturalizing has always involved the hard sciences. Historical, ethnographic, and sociological methods do not look like the tools of a naturalizer. Although it is true that cultural approaches do not employ the natural sciences in their analysis, they remain broadly naturalistic on my terms because they refuse to let knowledge float entirely free of the world. They look at the cultural context in which the mind has been operating in order to understand why beliefs have taken their particular shape. This is consistent with Quine's original suggestion that it is better to investigate how knowledge does in fact proceed by looking empirically at the actual details, rather than to fabricate a fictitious structure to similar effect. This is a watered-down sense in which those who use cultural methods are still naturalizers. They still are concerned with the situating of knowledge.

But even granted certain basic-level commonalities, there are significant tensions between cultural and scientific naturalizers that should be acknowledged at the outset. The cultural approach has close affinities to the poststructuralist position that language and social practice are largely responsible for how the world appears to us. This view insists that we are unable to attain any context-free view of things. For this reason, cultural naturalizers are often suspicious of scientific naturalizers because the former question whether the turn to biology and cognitive science can really tell us anything about the world that is not bound up in the language games of particular cultures and practices. Cultural naturalizers typically doubt there can be an account of how cognition works that really gets to the facts of the matter because they are skeptical of the whole idea of there being any facts of the matter. Natural sciences appear to be too bound up in the modernist fantasies of absolute certainty to have a genuine role in knowledge projects. The natural sciences are therefore often the *target* of the critiques offered by cultural naturalizers. Scientific naturalizers, in turn, find the cultural approach too wrapped up in linguistic maneuvering and too academically detached to hold it in any kind of regard.

This tension between scientific and cultural naturalizers is extremely difficult to resolve, and it remains consistently in the background for the rest of the book. For now it is necessary only to make my first acknowledgment of the tension and to move on. For with or without the tension between the two approaches, it is instructive to trace how some of the cultural naturalizers have ended up in the same territory as some of the scientific naturalizers. Representatives of both groups have started to find that certain aspects of the physical environment are becoming impossible for epistemology to ignore.

Because science has often been assumed to offer the paradigm case of knowledge production, a good deal of cultural naturalizing considers the peculiar culture that surrounds the production of scientific knowledge. One of the earliest cultural approaches to naturalizing scientific knowledge was the historical method employed by Thomas Kuhn in his *Structure of Scientific Revolutions*. Though Kuhn never called himself a naturalizer, he fits the formula that Quine laid down because he looked historically at how science has in fact proceeded rather than engaging in armchair speculation about how he thought that it should proceed. Kuhn considered a number of major theoretical transitions in the history of science in order to make his case for the movement of science. Through a detailed consideration of the actual circumstances of the theoretical breakthroughs made by such scientists as Copernicus, Newton, Lavoisier, and Einstein, Kuhn assembled a picture of science proceeding by periodic revolutions, followed by times of normality, then anomaly, then crisis, then further revolutions. Just a few years after Kuhn, Paul K. Feyerabend also employed detailed historical analysis of particular case studies to give his own account of how science proceeds. His historically situated discussions of Parmenides, Aristotle, Galileo, Priestley, Lorentz, and Maxwell illustrated that there are never solely rational reasons that determine exactly how one theory comes to be replaced by another. Feyerabend used this observation to argue for "anything goes" as the best methodology for the pursuit of scientific knowledge.

Kuhn and Feyerabend are on my terms two of the earliest cultural naturalizers. They made it clear that scientists do not stand outside of their theoretical and historical locations when they make their claims. Whereas Kuhn was concerned primarily with describing the process, Feyerabend was more interested in whether a person's historical and theoretical background would help or hinder the chance of progress being made. The historicism in both positions caused an immediate and strong reaction from their peers because it appeared to replace the idea of scientific progress with one of historical contingency. Yet compared to some of the other cultural naturalizers, the scope of Kuhn's and Feyerabend's naturalizing was actually relatively narrow. Once historians of science had identified the historical milieu in which scientists operated, they had said most of what there was to say about how scientists' cultural location might affect their beliefs.

A second strain of the cultural approach contains perhaps the largest volume of literature. This can be usefully called the "sociological" strain. Broadly speaking, these theorists look at the interests and values contained in the particular social context of those involved in the production of knowledge for clues as to why scientific theories take one form rather than another. Though these social values are never completely separable from the theoretical milieu with which Kuhn and Feyerabend were concerned, this second strain of naturalizing has the potential to add several more levels of situatedness to knowledge. Now there is not just the theoretical but also the social context of knowledge production to be investigated.

Taking into account this context means doing some sociology. In the last twenty-five years, there have been a growing number of retrospective sociological studies that have exposed the value biases inherent in work that originally passed as value-neutral, objective science. Some of these studies have their roots in early 1970s feminist critiques that sought to eliminate male biases from scientific theory. Adrienne Zihlman, for example, exposed how man-the-hunter accounts of evolution are biased by the assumption that only men have the potential to cause evolutionary change. [21] Cynthia Russet and Stephen J. Gould have both shown how Victorian gender biases created and shaped the sciences of physiognomy and craniology. Nancy Stephan has completed a similar kind of analysis of Victorian studies of race, and Robert Proctor has exposed the value biases inherent in Nazi studies of medicine and of genetics.[22] Since it often takes somebody from outside the group to spot a bias, such studies are sure to proliferate as scientific communities become increasingly diverse along a number of axes.

In very few of these cases were the social values believed to have been brought into science deliberately. They filtered only very surreptitiously into work often specifically designed to exclude them. For this reason Lorraine Code refers to them as "hidden subjectivities."[23] Ruth Bleier agrees with Code that, whatever methodological precautions are in place, scientists still struggle to completely "hang their subjectivity up at the door."[24] Sandra Harding has helpfully pointed out how subjective value judgments can occur at several important junctures during scientific inquiry: the initial selection of problems, the formation of hypotheses, the design of research, the formation of research committees, the collection of data, the interpretation and sorting of data, decisions about when to stop research, and the way that results of research are reported.[25] Sociological investigations of knowledge are designed to reveal the particular social values that influenced these decisions. In order to become aware of when a scientist is introducing a value, Lorraine Code recommends "taking subjectivity into account" by pressing epistemologists to "pay as much attention to the nature and situation—the location—of [the agent] as they commonly pay to the content of her claim."[26] In a somewhat similar fashion, Harding suggests taking a "reflexive" approach to knowledge, one that looks back upon the scientist to search for hidden value biases that might be brought into his or her work.[27] Many of these theorists refer to a value-laden position in the world as an "epistemic location."

This sociological approach to uncovering value biases can be taken in some interesting directions. A more radical group of sociological naturalizers advocates what is known as "the strong program" in the sociology of scientific knowledge. The strong program, associated with Barry Barnes and David Bloor at the University of Edinburgh, goes beyond just looking for the biases in bad science. Sociologists in the strong program suggest that what is true of science that turns out to be bad is also true of science currently thought to be good. They advocate a symmetrical, sociological treatment of beliefs that are both in and out of favor. For Barnes and Bloor, epistemology can usefully engage in the sociological study of what it takes for a particular corpus of belief to triumph at a particular time.

Before moving onto a third group of cultural naturalizers, there are four important points to note about both the historical and sociological naturalizers in order to connect them into the story that I have started to tell about place and mind. First, both historical and sociological approaches challenge the belief in the passivity of the agent of knowledge by showing how facts about the agent's situation trickle into scientific research. The world alone is not determining belief. These positions contain the neo-Kantian synthesis of something brought by the world and something brought by the scientist. The second observation is that by stressing the importance of historical and social location, these theorists have moved away from not only the idea of a passive agent of knowledge but also the idea of a single, generic agent of knowledge. Historical and social locations are assumed to continually bring multiple different shapes to the knowledge claims of different groups of individuals. This is generally not the case for the naturalizers who use the scientific approach described above. The natural sciences tend to assume that the contribution of the mind is generic across all individuals. For the sociological and the historical naturalizers, by contrast, scientists are altered by each of the different contexts in which they reside. The third observation is that situating the agent of knowledge has increasingly meant looking not just at the agent of knowledge as an individual but also at the interactions the agent has with the environments in which he or she resides. In looking to what the individual brings to knowledge, one is forced to look back out at his wider context. For the historical naturalizers this context is a set of current scientific theories; for the sociological naturalizers it is a cultural milieu. In both cases, there is no such thing as an isolable individual knower. No ideas or experiences stuck in the individual's head and cut off from the world outside of it. No knowers in vats.

The final point is related to this third observation and is in the form of a gentle critique of the emphasis in the historical and sociological approaches. Of these four observations about the kinds of cultural naturalizing described so far, this last one is the most important for the trajectory of this book. Andrew Pickering notes how sociological approaches to the study of science have taken us considerably beyond Descartes by articulating how human agency plays an important role in creating the shape of scientific knowledge. Pickering believes that in doing so they have "partially displaced the representational [mirror] idiom by seeing the production, evaluation, and use of scientific knowledge as structured by the interests of and constraints upon real human agents."[28] The down side of this, according to Pickering, is that the success of the sociological approaches has led to the neglect of the active role also played by the physical world in creating a knowledge claim. Kant had insisted that knowledge was a synthesis of mind and world. Idealists erred in neglecting the world part of that synthesis. In similar fashion, the emphasis by sociologists on the presence of human agency in science has had the unintended effect of leading to "the invisibility of material agency."[29] Scientists, Pickering reminds us, act as they do in response to a physical world that does things to them and to their instruments. Sociologists of science have tended to forget this. The world itself becomes almost silent in the sociological analysis. Now that a new language of scientists who speak from particular epistemic locations has been created, it would certainly be ironic if these locations were to be understood only in the metaphorical sense of a social location. Presumably there are also aspects of a scientist's literal location among the physical forms filling the laboratory that add relevant shape to what he or she claims. These literal locations among the physical forms of the laboratory are what the third approach to cultural naturalizing describes.

This third strain of the cultural approach I call "materialist." The canonical text in this approach—an approach also known as lab studies—is Bruno Latour and Steve Woolgar's 1979 study *Laboratory Life: The Social Construction of Scientific Facts*. Adherents to this approach take as their starting point the fact that a scientist in a laboratory is not just engaged in representing nature; this scientist is also intervening in nature.[30] In addition to demanding particular skills from the scientists themselves, intervening in nature requires particular types of arrangements of instrumentation and experimental apparatus in the physical spaces of the lab. These arrangements are set up so that a particular part of nature's order can be highlighted and observed. In making it visible, the material arrangements of the lab inevitably make the object appear a certain way. Laboratory instruments serve to capture that appearance and transform it into some currency that is usable by the laboratory community.

Lab studies theorist Karin Knorr-Cetina draws from these facts about intervention the conclusion that the laboratory itself has become "an important agent of scientific development."[31] Using Merleau-Ponty's terminology, Knorr-Cetina points out that the laboratory supplies the phenomenal field in which experience is made in science. It is within this field that the system of "self-others-things" is created. Scientific theories are always products of "a particular reconfiguration of the natural order in relation to the social order."[32] This reconfiguration is a product of both human and material agency. A reconfigured phenomenal field requires the active participation of the lab every bit as much as it requires the active participation of the scientist. Knorr-Cetina's recognition of the role of the physicality of the lab is a significant addition to anything that was said in either the historical or the sociological approaches.

Pickering concurs. The error made by the sociological naturalizers of considering only human agency in the laboratory can be remedied, according to Pickering, by recognizing the material agency of the lab. He asks us to remember that "the world . . . is continually doing things, things that bear upon us not as observation statements upon disembodied intellects but as forces upon material beings . . . think of the weather."[33] Instruments in the lab are vehicles with which to "capture, seduce, download, recruit" that material agency. Knowledge, he says, is "threaded through the machinic field of science," the product of what he calls the "mangle of practice" (7). Science must always be open to recognizing "the constitutive intertwining [that] exists between material and human agency" (15). Laboratory studies should never be satisfied with sociology alone. In the intertwining of people and nature, the material is at least as vital as the human. There is a "dance of agency" in the lab.

From Pickering's description of a dance of agency between human and material actors, it should be clear that lab studies theorists do not leave the sociological naturalizers completely behind. They insist that the lab be regarded simultaneously as a richly social, cultural, and physical environment. Techniques used in the lab create an order of nature that is both natural and social, something that Donna Haraway has called the material-semiotic.[34] In Knorr-Cetina's words, "scientific objects are not only 'technically' manufactured in laboratories but are also inextricably symbolically or politically construed" through such things as the political alliances that scientific communities create and the forms of persuasion they employ.[35] More than any of the other theorists discussed in this chapter, lab studies theorists seem willing to acknowledge the simultaneous play of the social and the physical. Lab studies thus become a gateway into a rich and complex account of the construction of knowledge that includes both social and material actors. Unlike the sociologists and the historicists, the lab studies theorists never emphasize human and social agency in knowledge construction to the extent that they forget the equally important material agency. The most significant insight that materialist naturalizers maintain is to insist that the material environment is always active and involved alongside the activity of the persons manufacturing knowledge.

The distinctions I have made between historical, sociological, and material strains of the cultural approach are fairly roughly made cuts through a tangled mass of theories. Moreover, the tangle is getting bigger at an impressive rate.[36] The thread that connects all three approaches together is the commitment to using a cultural analysis to situate the agent (or agents) of knowledge. Despite the tangle of theories, there are two important trends to notice. First, the Platonic and modernist approaches to knowledge that were demonized in chapter 1 are nowhere in sight. The neo-Kantian view of knowledge as a synthesis between something brought by the scientist and something brought by the world is centrally incorporated. The Quinean improvement over Kant, that the scientist brings something about his or her attachment to the world rather than something about his or her transcendence of it, is also included. The scientific knowledge produced in the lab reflects actual historical, social, and material factors introduced through the scientist. This means that, for most of the cultural naturalizers, knowledge is neither hyper-pure nor alienated from the world in the glassy essence of a person's mind. It is always *in* the world, contextually located and available for historical, sociological, and material critique.

A second noteworthy point about the cultural approach is that since the early days with Kuhn and Feyerabend there has been a gradual expansion in the number of factors that have been treated as relevant components of an agent's epistemic location. The historical, the social, and the material situations of the agent of knowledge have each in turn been shown to be relevant in different versions of the cultural approach. Even just within the sociological approach, theorists such as Lorraine Code have identified race, gender, ethnicity, and class among the epistemic locations that an agent might bring to his or her knowledge claims. When lab studies and historical methods are added, several more levels of situatedness appear. Throughout the complex process of detailing the different aspects of a person's cultural location, agents of knowledge have been shown to be decreasingly generic and increasingly situated. Coming back down to earth about knowledge has involved forging a surprising number of constitutive connections between knowing minds and the worlds that they inhabit.

Grounding Environments

If there is a single lesson to be drawn from this brief look at the scientific and the cultural approaches to naturalizing, it is that both approaches have been inexorably driven to look back out from the individual making a knowledge claim in order to recognize the importance of the ambient environment to their theories. Environment has meant a number of things to each of the different theorists ranging from the biological brain to the skeleto-muscular body to the historical and theoretical milieu to the social environment and, finally, to the laboratory. In each case, the epistemologist has insisted upon a distinctive context from which individuals and communities construct their claims. Particularly suggestive is the fact that some of these theorists have found themselves increasingly having to include details of the concrete physical realities of the spaces in which knowledge makers operate as part of the relevant context. The neurotic and alienated mind that Latour identified needed first a therapeutic reconnection to the brain, then another to the body, and now, finally, its full healing seems to require a connection to the physical spaces in which those bodies roam. In the enactivist discussion, this became clear when it was recognized that understanding cognition required knowing something about embodied action. In the lab studies discussion, it became clear when theorists recognized the importance of the material agency of the lab. Richly situating knowledge, I suggest, requires continuing on down these paths. These are all paths that call for the grounding of knowledge.

If we are going to take seriously the grounding of knowledge, it will be important to consider what kinds of environments are going to supply the grounding. Under what conditions does an environment actually make a difference? The discussion started in the laboratory because the laboratory is widely regarded as the paradigmatic site of knowledge production. But the laboratory is far from the only place in which knowledge gets manufactured. Understanding what goes on in the scientific laboratory is not the only way to understand what happens when knowledge gets produced. We will not have a richly situated epistemology if we ignore the range of situations in which knowledge gets constructed. As Lorraine Code put this point, "naturalism cannot deliver on its promise . . . if it grants uncontested pride of place in its study of natural knowledge to behaviors studied in the laboratory."[37]

An encouraging trait of the lab studies theorists is that they often appear willing to move their analyses outside the lab and into other kinds of environments. Latour seems reluctant to limit the lab to some kind of bricks and mortar enclosure. He denies that any laboratory is hermetically sealed off from what lies outside, insisting instead that "no one can say where the lab is and where society is."[38] He illustrates how Louis Pasteur's experiments with the anthrax virus problematized the final determination of where the lab begins and ends. Since half of Pasteur's experiments took place on the farm, Latour argues that the inside/outside boundary for a laboratory does not always work well. In *Pandora's Hope,* Latour's laboratory studies analysis takes place on the edge of a forest in Brazil.

Knorr-Cetina also wants to take her analysis outside the lab. She has already recommended that lab studies theorists extend their research to "the clinic, the factory, the garden, and the government agency." She suggests that what has been learned from lab studies can be applied "to larger questions about the localization of experience in multiply embedded and varied sites." She wonders "what different patterns emerge when we consider these sites in regard to their epistemic relations to an environment."[39] Ed Hutchins has recently provided some answers to this question in an analysis of how knowledge gets constructed on a navy ship.[40]

The analysis can be taken outside the lab because at the bottom of the lab studies insight about material agency lies a very general point indeed. Knorr-Cetina gives a clue about this point in a footnote in which she remarks, "a culture in which artificial light is available will have a means of extending the day and as a consequence will experience the world differently than a culture without artificial light."[41] This makes a room with artificial light into a primitive kind of laboratory that offers an epistemically useful reconfiguration of the phenomenal field. If simply switching on a light can do this, then what other sorts of interventions into the order of things have the same potential? Presumably a great many of them. This suggests the much more general insight that there is often something epistemically significant going on in situations that involve even the smallest reconfigurations of the relationship between self and world. These reconfigurations can involve something as complex as illuminating a proton with a laser beam or something as simple as turning on a light. But if the insight is this general, it seems unlikely that it can be restricted to only human interventions into the natural order.

Though some reconfigurations of the wider phenomenal field clearly involve human intervention, others presumably do not. Pickering asked us to think of the weather. Walking outside on a morning when snow has fallen during the night presents a considerable reconfiguration of the phenomenal field. In that reconfigured world, things appear dramatically different. Not only the landscape but also the walker are transformed. The walker's hearing is more acute and vision a little less reliable as he or she adjusts to the different lines and colors of the snow-covered world. The walker's body moves to a different rhythm in an attempt to get every shred of friction that worn-out boots can generate. These significant reconfigurations suggest that the lab studies lessons might in reality be much broader lessons about how knowing in general always occurs in concert with the particulars of our physical environments. In other words, we are constantly engaging with the details. We do not live in the general. Pickering was right to point out that "much of everyday life has this character of coping with material agency."[42] The physical world continually acts to supply us with particular perspectives on its arrangement. So there is a general point to be extracted from lab studies: reconfigurations of the phenomenal field of self-other-world are taking place almost the whole time that knowledge is being made, both inside and outside the laboratory.

Once we are comfortable with taking the general lab studies insight outside the laboratory, there are numerous different types of environments we might consider for their relevance to knowledge production. The home, the workplace, and the city immediately come to mind as constructed environments with considerable agency in the knowledge claims that individuals and societies make. Although these environments will be an important part of richly situated epistemologies, it should be obvious that I am more interested in the epistemic effects of environments that show less sign of being constructed by humans. My own biases as an environmentalist at this point call me back out of the epistemological analysis of artifactual environments and into the wild. What can we make of the material agency of a salt marsh? In what ways does the high arctic shape thought? What is the epistemic significance of the temperate rainforest? Or a high plains blizzard? If, as Knorr-Cetina suggested, artificial light is enough to reconfigure the relation of self-others-things, then torrential downpours, fast-flowing rivers, and the presence of grizzly bears are all likely to do the same things in equally significant ways. In fact, I suspect that the reconfiguration of the phenomenal field is at least as apparent in wild nature, for example, when you step onto a fishing boat and head out into a storm, as it is when you step from a classroom and into a laboratory. There are several times in each day when even the most office-bound among us finds the phenomenal field reconfigured through direct or indirect contact with the spontaneity of the natural world.

I find these questions about the agency of natural environments interesting, partly, no doubt, because I just like being in them. This is one of the not-very-well-hidden subjectivities I bring to my own claims. But my interest in these questions is also very much informed by the belief that human ecological rootedness in the natural environment, though now often obscured by artifice, is still a deeply important part of who we are. We still like to breathe cold, clean air, to walk along riverbanks in the fall, and to hike to the top of steep hills when we are feeling fit. We still shiver in a cold wind, steel ourselves against winter's early morning darkness, and listen to our cellular tissues hum on contact with the warmth of the sun's rays on the early days of spring. It is not just that we still like to engage with the natural environment in our daily lives; we also have a deep historical contact with those environments. We are creatures who evolved into environments that looked much more like the Badlands of South Dakota than suburban Portland. Our upright posture is still useful for many of the same reasons that it was when it evolved in the early hominids in the Rift Valley of East Africa. Our opposable thumbs and our arms now do many things that they did not do when we first gained them, but they are still useful for a lot of the reasons for which they were originally useful, such as for picking things up off the ground and holding on to people tightly. If it is the case, as Piaget suggested, that some of our image schemas are innate, then these schemas presumably emerged out of interactions with the physical environments in which we evolved. These environments are our historic home and thus have a deep historical involvement in the way that thought works. Through this involvement they also still have, at some distant level perhaps, an influence on the knowledge claims that we make.

As I hope this chapter makes clear, there are already a few places in which the significance of physical environment to knowledge and belief has begun to appear in contemporary epistemology. The next two chapters marshal different kinds of evidence for the claim that knowing involves a complex, dialectical relationship between agents of knowledge and the environments in which they reside. Such controversial claims require support from a number of different arenas. It is time to venture just a little further afield to find support for the grounding of knowledge.

I only went out for a walk, and finally concluded
to stay out until sundown, for going out,
I really found I was going in.

John Muir, *The Story of My Boyhood and Youth*

3 ORGANISMS AND ENVIRONMENTS

When John Muir stepped out into the wilderness, what he
found there was a curious reflection of himself, a personhood that both was
and was not his own. Nature presented to his senses something that he felt
was already incorporated deep within the structures of his experience. In going out, he found that he was really going in. What are we to make of this
enigmatic claim from one of America's greatest wilderness advocates? Is Muir
caught up in an illusion that causes him to romantically project a union between self and world in the face of his obvious aesthetic interest in nature? Or is
he reaching toward the important insight that the processes traditionally taken
to be inner workings of the human mind are in fact intimately connected with
the physical spaces around us? Did Muir himself recognize there are important
connections between place and mind—the same insight that has led ecocritic
Scott Slovic to refer to nature writers as "literary psychologists"?[1]

While the previous chapter looked for hints in existing epistemologies and
cognitive sciences that physical environments are important to our under-
standings of thought and belief, the next two chapters range a little wider.
The case needs to be made as widely as possible because the evidence from

within any single discipline such as cognitive science or laboratory studies is only fledgling in form. Given the depth of the tradition we have inherited, any proposal to reduce the alienation between mind and world is controversial. Just reattaching the mind to the body has been a tough enough sell for people such as Johnson. So although we are in a better position today to make the case for a richly situated knowledge than either Quine or Shepard was, there is still not yet enough evidence in place to make a compelling and complete argument from within any one discipline. It will take a considerable shift in how we look at the relationship between organism and environment across a number of disciplines if thought and belief are to be brought back down to earth. So the strategy for the next two chapters is to construct a broad, synthetic case for the connections between place and mind. The goal is to produce enough breadth in argument to eventually prompt epistemologists to follow Ed Hutchins's directive and articulate "an ecology of thinking in which human cognition interacts with an environment rich in organizing resources."[2]

A small note of caution before proceeding. Chapters 3 and 4 employ the distinction used in chapter 2 between scientific and cultural approaches to naturalizing knowledge. This chapter focuses exclusively on making a scientific case and chapter 4 on making a cultural case. Though the distinction is cautiously retained as a way of splitting up the chapters, it should serve as only a weak endorsement of its viability. I have already pointed out that considerable tension exists between the two approaches. Those who take a cultural approach think that you cannot do science without talking about social values. But these cultural studies theorists are themselves ridiculed by those committed to a scientific path for how they appear to lack any commitment to knowledge of an independently existing reality outside of a social setting.[3] Given this complex and tense relationship between scientific and cultural approaches, why seal them up in separate chapters and refuse to engage the tension between them? I think that there are pragmatic reasons to include some arguments from the natural sciences that self-consciously avoid any kind of consideration of social and cultural values. People still find the idea of value-free science compelling. Scientific knowledge is still regarded paradigmatically as a set of timeless and universal representations of how the world actually is. The predictive power of the sciences that operate according to this paradigm continues to be impressive. Given that this is the context in which current environmental debates take place, there is a particular persuasive power in arguments for grounding knowledge that are still rooted firmly in the natural sciences. So for pragmatic reasons, I again relegate the tension to the background and start with some exclusively scientific arguments in favor of connecting place and mind. The first piece of scientific evidence is in the form of some broad brush strokes from evolutionary biology.

Dialectical Biology

It should be clear by now that any attempt to reconnect environment and belief is going to demand a radical departure from modernist views. One of the major differences between the approaches that I attempted to discredit in the first chapter and the postmodern views highlighted in the second is that the former insisted that everything there is to know about the environment is in principle knowable independently of whoever or whatever is doing the knowing. Modernist views assumed an extrinsic environment supplying a number of independently existing inputs that the organism proceeded to codify in the form of ideas or propositions and then returned to the environment as outputs in the form of behavior and knowledge claims. The postmodern views deny that the mind can be processing pregiven inputs and returning them as outputs to an autonomous environment because those very inputs are already shaped by the peculiarities of the organism-environment complex. In the enactivist approach used by such theorists as Piaget and Johnson, the environment is already shaped by the cognitive structures of the organism during experience. In the lab studies approach used by such theorists as Pickering, Latour, and Knorr-Cetina, material and human agency intertwine at every moment to present particular reconfigurations of the natural order in relation to the knowledge claimant.

Such postmodern accounts of knowledge challenge the idea that environment is wholly extrinsic to the cognizing organism. They demand the rejection of the view that organism and environment can be wholly isolated from one another. According to Varela, Thompson, and Rosch, enactivists have to "call into question the idea that information exists ready-made in the world and that it is extracted by a cognitive system."[4] The neo-Kantian approaches we have been exploring require that the notion of a world extrinsic to the cognizing system be replaced with the notion of a world integrally linked to the cognitive processes the organism continually employs. A corollary of this view is that it is no longer possible to imagine pulling the organism out of the environment and understanding everything about how it creates knowledge through an examination of it in that isolated state.

Hidden behind these views of how knowledge claims get made is a wider recasting of the relationship between organism and environment that reaches beyond questions of thought and belief. A close inspection of what is happening in the enactivist account reveals not just the organism's thoughts being shaped by sensorimotor action but the environment itself in some sense being reconfigured by the organism. Since an organism's environment is always lent shape by how he or she perceives it, the organism does not so much *experience* an external environment as *have* one of his or her own. Environments are *enacted* by organisms as they go about their daily activities. This deeper revisioning that enactivism requires suggests there is a more general story to be told about how to look at the relationship between organism and environment that reaches beyond anything in cognitive science and epistemology. This more general story is told in evolutionary biology by Richard Levins and Richard Lewontin.

Levins and Lewontin offer dialectical biology as an alternative to the standard adaptationist interpretation of Darwinian evolutionary biology. According to the adaptationist interpretation, organisms with randomly mutating genes get selected by environments when they stumble into pre-existing ecological niches. The environment, which is taken to be wholly extrinsic to the organism, is assumed to contain certain problems that the genes inside the organism endeavor to "solve." The environment is already fixed in what it offers, and the organism has to find a place amid the fixity in which it can survive. In this view, those organisms that survive are those whose "morphological, physiological and behavioral traits represent the best solutions to the problems."[5] Finding itself a comfortable niche becomes the primary task for a successfully evolving organism.

This adaptationist view has certain implications for how we look at different aspects of the relation between organism and environment. One of the first implications is that the organism and environment are ascribed an extraordinary level of independence from each other. The organism is born into a pre-existing environment and then has to use a combination of its wits and its random genetic mutations to find the niche in which it can best survive. In adaptationism, neither organism nor environment can significantly change each other in the current generation. The environment already contains pre-existing problems such as limited food sources, impediments to locomotion, and extremely cold temperatures. Either the random mutations of the genes inside the organism solve the problem in a future generation, or these environmental conditions bring about the death of the species in a timely fashion. "Adapt or die" is the chilling adaptationist injunction. So, for example, the problem-pressed proto-penguin underwent some lucky mutations and added a food group, some webbing between the toes, and a thick layer of blubber that eventually enabled it to survive in the Antarctic. The dinosaurs, similarly imperiled by environmental conditions beyond their control, were not so lucky. Malthusian pressures are plainly evident in Darwin's characterization of evolution as a matter of imperiled individuals suffering horrendous fates in the face of limiting environmental conditions.

This adaptationist account assumes that the environment has sole responsibility for supplying the problems and that the organism and its subsequent generations have sole responsibility for solving them. The organism either finds itself a niche in which it is adapted to the problems, migrates elsewhere toward a different set of problems, or dies out. Environments are like gently inclined planes with carefully sized holes cut into them. Organisms through evolutionary time are like spheres rolling down those planes. The organisms either find a pre-existing hole in which to settle, subtly change direction through a mutation and blunder into a hole, or miss all the opportunities to arrest their fall and roll helplessly off the end of the plane and into oblivion. The important thing that the adaptationist picture leaves out is any possibility that an organism might transform its environment and the problems presented to it in order to settle somewhere other than where the holes have already been cut in the plane. Adaptationism does not allow organism and environment to influence each other in advance of the selection pressures. They are just thrown in the ring together to make of each other what they can.

This alienation of organism from environment appears again through a different lens in adaptationism's view of the causal relationship between the organism and the evolutionary forces. Adaptationism completely eliminates any role for the flesh-and-blood organism in the mechanics of evolution. The forces that determine survival are provided entirely by the gene on the one hand and by the environment on the other. Genes produce phenotypes that may or may not survive, and environments supply conditions that can prove to be fatal or accommodating. Organisms unfold according to a predetermined genetic plan, and environments either kill the organisms or let the genes survive and replicate. In the case of both survival and extinction, the whole organism is the object of forces acting independently of it and has no subjectively determined role to play in the causal process. In the technical language of dialectical biology, the shape of the organism is determined "heteronomously," from environment on the outside and from genes deep on the inside. Levins and Lewontin describe this as a placing of the organism "at the nexus of internal and external forces, each of which has its own laws, independent of each other and of the organism that is their creation" (88). The organism has little of evolutionary significance to do for itself. It is merely the medium through which these two other forces act. As a result, the study of evolution is reduced to a combination of molecular biology and ecology. In *The Selfish Gene*, Richard Dawkins reveals the impact of this view when he characterizes the organism as a lumbering robot, a vehicle completely controlled by the efforts of its genes to replicate themselves.

When you contemplate the implications of this view, it seems somewhat odd, to say the least, for the organism to be contributing so little to one of the universe's most subtle pieces of mechanics. The organism is the macrolevel entity that actually does things in the world. It breaks off branches to reach succulent leaves, it makes a bed to rest in, and it chooses a mate with whom to produce offspring. But according to the adaptationist picture, it is not doing anything to help or hinder its evolutionary fate because that fate has already been determined by its adapted or ill-adapted genes. Such a deterministic view leaves the organism out in the evolutionary cold. It seems a little surprising that the organism does not have any hand in its own evolutionary future. Dialectical biology begins its challenge to the adaptationist view by insisting that the organism counts for something in the evolutionary process.

A first point of departure of dialectical biology from adaptationism is that the former denies that organisms can be reduced to the product of just two forces, genes and environment. Levins and Lewontin are critical of the degree of determination ascribed to the gene in the adaptationist account. They do not accept that organisms simply unfold according to a plan preinscribed in their DNA limited only by the constraints of their environment. Even though they accept the idea that a phenotype is influenced causally by the genotype, they deny that it is absolutely determined by it. Nor do they think that the addition of the environmental conditions enables a full determination of what the organism will look like. There is more to evolution than genes and environments. Lewontin uses his studies of differences between fruit flies as evidence that "even if I knew the genes of a developing organism and the complete sequence of its environments, I could not specify the organism."[6] He argues that the number of bristles that develop under the left and right wings of fruit flies are not just the result of genes and of environment but are also due to the contributions of individual flies themselves. These contributions take the form of "variation in the growth and division of cells during development" (27). This developmental noise ensures that organisms with the same genotype and the same environment vary considerably. "It is a fundamental principle of development genetics," claims Lewontin, "that every organism is the outcome of a unique interaction between genes and environmental sequences modulated by the random chances of cell growth and division" (27).

This means that the organism itself, in addition to its genes, has a hand in its own future. "At every moment," say Levins and Lewontin, "gene, environment, chance, and the organism as a whole are all participating."[7] This part of their argument resurrects the importance of the organism in evolution. Organisms are not "the passive objects of external forces, but the creators and modulators of these forces" (104). This move is significant because the organism ceases to be entirely passive, a product solely of environmental conditions and genetic inheritance. The organism gains in dialectical biology by becoming an active player in creating an evolutionary tension. Levins and Lewontin describe this as making the organism into both the "subject and object of evolution."

Having first reactivated the organism in the evolutionary process, Levins and Lewontin next re-engage the organism with its environment. They point out that a second mistake in the adaptationist picture is its assumption that the external environment is a completely autonomous entity that exerts predetermined forces on an organism. The adaptationist view sponsored the image of an organism born into a pre-existing environment desperately needing to find a niche in which it can survive. The problem with this interpretation becomes apparent when one asks what these niches would look like before the organism arrives. Posing the question this way makes it evident that there can be no such thing as a niche antecedent to an organism filling it. Niches, the dialectical biologist points out, are not holes precut into the surface of the earth into which wandering organisms can settle. They are, in fact, places created by organisms from among an infinite number of possibilities that are not specified ahead of time. Even though they could be potential niches, Levins and Lewontin point out that no birds eat the leaves from the tops of trees and no animal crawls on its stomach, lays eggs, and eats grass. The niche for a particular bird has to be defined contextually by "a list of what the bird eats, of what and where it builds its nest, how much time it spends foraging in different parts of the trees or ground, what its courtship pattern is and so on" (98). A niche is not a prefurnished home, generously supplied by an already designed environment, but a pattern of activity of a given organism. In an important sense, the environment of an organism does not exist as an isolable, independent entity. It has to be described in concert with the activities of the organism that survives there.

Levins and Lewontin use a number of illustrations to make their point about these integral organism-environment relations. They draw attention to the fact that thrushes use the stones at the base of trees to break snail shells while woodpeckers have no use for the same stones. They describe how organisms change the environment with which they interact through ecological succession. They remark on how the arrival of different soil microbes can dramatically change the composition of the soil in an area and on how a good berry year can result in large increases in the populations of certain fauna. They also point out that individual organisms create for themselves special microclimates in which they can more easily survive through strategies such as layering themselves in hair to trap warm air near the skin. In each of these cases, the organism is literally creating the environment in which it can survive, not waiting until it wanders or mutates into a viable relationship with one. It has become a truism of ecological theory that old ecological accounts of climax ecosystems and ecological stability missed the fact that ecosystems function more through disturbance and change than through stasis. Dialectical biology goes out of its way to point out that these changes result not just from earthquake, fire, and flood but also from the continuous activities of billions of organisms transforming their environments as they go about their daily and seasonal economies. Root fungi kill entire forests, and mule deer browse whole hillsides bare. Organisms do not *find* niches so much as *create* them.

The strong message to take away from dialectical biology is that organism and environment are entities much more tightly bound to each other than adaptationism had appreciated. An environment is not just the space that surrounds an organism and supplies it with a fixed number of predetermined stimuli; it is something that can be understood only relative to the activities and characteristics of the organism itself. As Levins and Lewontin put it, " 'environment' cannot be understood merely as surroundings, no matter how dynamically. It is also a way of life" (58). The environment of an organism is not "an autonomous process but a reflection of the biology of the species" (99). The emphasis can also be placed the other way. The organism is defined in part by its activities in an environment. And the organism is not just a passive object of evolutionary forces created by its environment but is itself a modulator of those forces. In articulating these much tighter connections between organism and environment, dialectical biology places a special emphasis on process and activity. Environments are not independent entities experienced by an organism but ways of living, enacted by organisms even as the organisms continue to be shaped by their environments. Adaptationism, by contrast, does not do justice to the dynamic integration of organism and environment. In place of adaptationism's alienation of organism from environment, dialectical biology paints a picture of the two as actively co-determining each other at every moment. Levins and Lewontin recommend that the metaphor of adaptation be replaced by the metaphor of mutual construction. The organism is always mutually enfolded and in reciprocal evolutionary tension with its environment.

My own interest lies less with what dialectical biology says we should think about evolution and more with the implications this account has for cognition and for knowledge production. Though it is perhaps not possible to import all the lessons of dialectical biology directly into epistemology and cognitive science, it is important to consider what kind of lessons these might be. Dialectical biology says something powerful about the organism-environment relation, and knowledge is, after all, just one aspect of this relationship. Creating theories and beliefs is something that organisms do through interactions with their environments.

Though dialectical biology does not say anything directly about epistemology, it includes some hints about its implications for theories of knowledge. Dialectical biologists note how organisms respond to their environments by amplifying and transforming certain signals and by suppressing others. Canids have evolved to amplify olfactory cues while placing less emphasis on visual ones. The enhancement of different sensory skills means that the world each organism experiences is essentially a different world. There is no single environment perceived by all species. Moreover, this is not just a reflection of differences in sensory ability. Organisms not only have different ways of sensing the environment; in some cases the forces available to be sensed literally change depending on the organism. Features particular to each organism can determine which "universal" laws of nature it experiences. A bacterium suspended in a liquid is too small to be affected by the force of gravity yet is the right size to be affected by Brownian motion. Similarly, gravity is not a force that most fish need to worry about. In each case, particulars of the organism determine the world it experiences and in which it lives.

Through these integral connections between organism and environment, dialectical biology seems to confirm that modernist approaches to knowledge are biologically inadequate. In their book on the embodied mind, Varela, Thompson, and Rosch point out how accepting dialectical biology means rejecting the modernist idea of correspondence between ideas and the world because of the separation between organism and environment that correspondence theory entails. Recognizing the implications of dialectical biology for modernist epistemology, the authors state that "representationalism in cognitive science is the precise homologue of adaptationism in evolutionary theory."[8] Any demise of the latter signals a similar fate for the former. This suggests that naturalizers in epistemology should take their lead from Levins and

Lewontin and refuse to regard the organism as the passive object of forces external to it when it sets out to create knowledge. The organism does not simply sit back and receive stimuli from an autonomous environment. Descartes, Locke, the logical positivists, and the cognitivists were wrong about this. The organism modulates those stimuli through its engaged and embodied action in the world. The organism cooperates with the environment in constructing beliefs at the same time as the environment is shaping what and how the organism knows. Dialectical biology strongly suggests a dialectical approach to knowledge. Not only are agents epistemically active, but environments are, too. Organism and environment actively co-determine each other not only physically but also cognitively.

There does, of course, appear to be a significant difference between the projects of postmodern epistemologists and those of dialectical biologists. The former are talking about the construction of knowledge, and the latter are talking about the construction of organisms and environments. It would not be unreasonable to suggest that all the ontology talk should be kept separate from all the epistemology talk. The study of being has traditionally been regarded as demanding a different kind of inquiry from the study of knowing. But an interesting implication of dialectical biology is the softening of this very distinction between knowing and being. Dialectical biology does this by subscribing to a view of knowing not so much as an organism *representing* an external world as an organism *having* a world in which it can successfully operate. Dialectical biology suggests that knowing is a kind of activity or performance rather than the creation of a mental map of how the world is. It supports Mark Johnson's description of cognition as "a matter of an organism's embodiment . . . of perceptual mechanisms, patterns of discrimination, motor programs and various bodily skills."[9] Knowledge is not a static mental state but an ongoing process of being able to function in an environment that continually exerts its energy and forces upon the organism.

If knowing is connected directly to physical activity in an environment, it must be a mistake to investigate it entirely as the grasping of propositions about the world held in the head. Such a view suggests too impoverished an account of the knowledge process. If dialectical biology tells us that neither the organism nor the environment can be understood without considering the active co-determination of each other, then it is unlikely that activities such as knowing can be considered to take place without some of the same co-determination. If organism and environment are mutually enfolded in the provision of food and the construction of shelters, then they are perhaps similarly enfolded in the provision of thought and the construction of theories.

Although it should be pretty clear that dialectical biology is consistent with a view of cognition as an organism enacting for itself a world while in conversation with that world, clearly a lot more needs to be said to strengthen the case. [10] Several pieces are missing before we can confidently make the jump from a dialectical relationship between organism and environment in evolutionary biology to a similar dialectic in epistemology. The brush strokes offered so far in this chapter are a little too broad. Making the link between biology and knowing requires an argument to show that thought and knowledge really are much like the other activities of the organism, such as the use of the rocks to break open snail shells by the thrush or the eating of leaves at the top of the tree by the insects. What is needed is a theory that takes some of the insights contained in dialectical biology and applies them to some of the more specialized activities of animals, such as perception and thought. For this we can start by turning to James J. Gibson's ecological approach to visual perception. [11]

The Ecological Approach to Visual Perception

Gibson's account of visual perception is consistent with the organism-environment relation articulated in dialectical biology, and at the same time it adds solid support to the idea that physical environments play a constitutive role in activities normally considered the unique province of the mind. Gibson was not always as explicit as Levins and Lewontin about the ontology of the organism and environment relation, but he articulated an account of perception that draws on the mutual enfolding of both. By moving the discussion from ontology to perception, Gibson serves as a bridge figure between evolutionary biologists and the epistemologists. Since Plato's *Theaetetus,* epistemologists have recognized a close relationship between knowledge and perception. The story that connects dialectical biology, the Gibsonian approach to visual perception, and the enactivist account of cognition takes full advantage of this close relationship.

Gibson's ecological psychology can in some lights be considered an attempt to rescue psychology from its own schizophrenia. For most of the twentieth century, psychology had struggled with the "two worlds" legacy that Descartes had bequeathed. By separating everything into the distinct worlds of mental substance and physical substance, Descartes had given to psychologists, scientists of the mind, the difficult task of having to straddle the material and the mental worlds. Psychology found itself with the dilemma of having to connect subjective accounts of phenomena with objective accounts of events in the physical world. The languages demanded by each were completely different and often incompatible with each other. A contemporary ecological psychologist articulates the dilemma as follows: "insofar as it is scientific, psychology must be about bodies as distinct from minds; and, insofar as it is about mental states, psychology cannot hope to be scientific in the explanatory sense."[12] Gibson's ecological approach to perception was an attempt to offer an account that starts to use the same vocabulary for both. It worked by studying perception not as a completely internal mental activity but as an embodied activity of an organism in an environment. It offered a retreat from the modernist radical separation of mental and physical substances and reconnected perception to an organism's ability to be animate in its world.[13]

Gibson's influential study focused on visual perception. As he began his study of vision, Gibson questioned his own earlier views that to understand visual perception one just had to know something about the brain and then something about the inputs it received though visual images on the retina.[14] He began to realize that vision was more complicated than that. His position in *The Ecological Approach to Visual Perception* adopted a much more systems-oriented approach. He claimed that vision depended "on the eyes in the head on a body supported by the ground."[15] Seeing involved the operation of a whole visual system that continually engages the world in dynamic ways. Gibson thought that trying to understand vision by placing images in front of a subject seated in a laboratory and talking about visual stimuli was to give an artificially restricted account of what seeing was all about. In his view, vision included looking around, walking up to interesting things, and moving oneself around objects to get different perspectives on them. Vision was a richly embodied activity, an achievement of flesh-and-blood beings in a particular environment. Vision was not about sitting passively and waiting for the senses to be acted upon. The emphasis was firmly upon embodied action in an environment. This was the ecological component of Gibson's approach.

The importance of an image on the retina was not altogether denied by Gibson. The retina was certainly still stimulated by patterns of light. But Gibson claimed that it was a mistake to think that seeing was entirely a matter of how the organism went about processing those retinal stimulations. To think as much was to fall prey to power of the metaphor of the retina as a projection screen looked upon by some inner mind's eye. Gibson characterized this mistaken view as one of the most seductive fallacies in the history of psychology. It was a similar kind of ghost-in-the-machine thinking that misled Descartes and Locke into positing the existence of a mind's eye that could look critically upon the impressions gained via the senses. But if, as Gibson thought, it was wrong to look at vision as beginning and ending with the sensing of an image on the retina, then clearly seeing would have to be accounted for in terms of something much broader. To achieve this, Gibson took the study of vision outside of the eye and back into the world beyond.[16]

Gibson posited the presence of an "optic array" from which an organism gathered environmental information. The optic array was made up of all the light present in the visual field made available both directly from the sun and indirectly through the reflection of light between objects. At any particular point in space light converged from all these ambient sources and created a particular pattern. The pattern presented itself to the organism in the form of a series of surfaces. Move just a little from that particular point, and the surfaces changed. Gibson suggested that in order to see, organisms had to actively sample the information contained in the optic array and determine the invariances that could be found there. Gathered from within this array, environmental information was not a fixed packet that an organism took on board in the form of a stimulus; it was the result of a dynamic path that the organism tracked through the world. The array could not then be described solely in the language of physics or optics; such descriptions had to be supplemented by an ecological account of the activity of the organism's exploring relationships. Environmental information was a much richer concept than sensory stimulus; it was so rich, according to Gibson, that the whole of empirical psychology should be an investigation of the activities determining how this information is picked up, rather than of some supposed internal mental transformation of fixed and discrete sensory stimuli.

Gibson's solution to psychology's schizophrenia made vision into an active process of linking the whole organism directly to the information it found as it moved around its environment. Eyes, he claimed, "go into activity in the presence of stimulus information."[17] Eyes were just one component of an integrated perceptual system that did the seeing. And though the stimulation of sense receptors certainly occurred during vision, that stimulation alone was not sufficient for seeing. There was a whole eye-head-body-brain system participating. Two contemporary Gibsonians made this clear when they stressed that the ecological approach to perception is one in which "information . . . is *obtained by*, not *presented to* organisms" (emphasis added).[18] The idea of vision as essentially a matter of processing stimuli is rejected. During ongoing embodied interactions, information is actively obtained from the environment by the perceptual system in the form of a flowing, ambient array of energy. Seeing a table, then, is not a matter of processing photons of light on the retina but of discovering a certain type of structure in the environment by moving through the optic array.

The shift of the explanatory emphasis from events behind the eyeball to events outside the skin of the perceiving organism seems like an extraordinarily counterintuitive idea to propose about perception when viewed through a modernist lens. But the shift begins to look a little less odd if Gibson's approach is considered alongside some of the lessons learned from dialectical biology. As it was for the dialectical biologists, for Gibsonians, the optic array sampled by the perceiving organism is something that can be understood only in relation to the organism's activities. With a phrase that looks like it could have come straight out of Levins and Lewontin's work, Gibson states, "the words animal and environment make an inseparable pair . . . each term implies the other."[19] Organisms are inevitably immersed in physical surroundings that provide both the context and the possibilities for the activities in which they engage. The Gibsonian approach entails that just as dialectical biology insisted that you cannot understand the nature of the organism without thinking about its relationships to its environment, so you cannot understand the nature of the organism's perception without considering those same relationships. Seeing is an organism-environment production and must be understood in terms of an ongoing dynamic activity rather than as the processing of a snapshot of some stimuli appearing on an internal movie screen.

Thinking of the organism and environment as inseparable led Gibson to propose that the information the organism picks up from the optic array is in the form of "affordances," which he describes as "what [the environment] offers the animal, what it provides or furnishes, whether for good or ill" (127). They are presentations of how the environment might offer a particular kind of engaged relationship with the organism. Hence an affordance is not just an extrinsic physical property of the world, but a unified set of possibilities relative to the specific activities of the organism being considered. For example, a table might afford a cat a surface on which to sit, a roof under which to take shelter, or a post on which to scratch claws. The same table might afford a human a surface on which to eat dinner and a place upon which to rest one's feet, but it is unlikely to afford the human a post on which to scratch nails. Only if the environmental information is an affordance for the organism can it meaningfully be perceived.[20]

Parsing vision in terms of affordances illustrates how the ecological account of perception continues to bind organism and environment together. To be an affordance, a pattern in the ambient array of information must persist and be meaningful for an organism. An ecological niche for a dialectical biologist starts to look like nothing more than a whole set of relatively persistent affordances for an ecological psychologist. Perception becomes a process that unites an organism with the useful things that the environment presents to that organism. It is an exploratory rather than a performative activity.[21]

The modernist wishing to prop up the old picture might still object that the perception of value-laden affordances comes only after the processing of retinal stimulations. But Gibson deals with this objection by insisting that affordances are perceived *directly* from the environment rather than inferred from sensory stimulations. Gibsonian Edward S. Reed gives an example of what is meant by the direct perception of an affordance:

> According to Gibson, one's awareness of the world, including its values, is direct. The fire looks dangerous because we can actually see that its heat and flames would burn us. We may have to learn to see such things, yet this learning is not a process of associating a sensed fire and a sensed burning into a representation of a dangerous fire, but a process of learning to pick up the information specifying the burning capacities of fires. Observers do not have to learn to construct representations of things or to associate sensations and representations with pleasurable outcomes. Observers do have to learn to make use of the information that is available to them in ways that are relevant to their activities and needs.[22]

The mature organism knows that a fire is dangerous. This knowledge is not a matter of an organism cognitively grasping a certain proposition or an idea, but the result of an organism having achieved a certain level of experiential familiarity with what its environment affords. The information actually exists in the environment and not in a head of some organism somewhere. The perception of an object or an event, says Gibson, is "an achievement of the individual, not an appearance in the theater of his consciousness."[23] This means looking at perception as an activity that enables an organism to keep in touch with the world in the broadest possible sense and not as the successful transfer of something initially outside the organism to some immaterial location on the inside.

By characterizing perception as a process of picking up possibilities directly from the environment, the traditional account of sensation starts to seem very hollow. Perceptual knowledge is less to do with our ability to sense things than with our ability to be animate among them. Gibson rejects the received view of perception as a matter of the passive receipt of something provided heteronomously from the environment. In its place, the ecological approach to perception implies that "to see things is to see how to get about among them and what to do or not do with them."[24]

If Gibson was right, then what he has shown is that it is impossible to talk about how an organism perceives without giving a detailed and particularized account of the environment within which that organism is acting. Perception hardly goes on inside the organism at all. It should be analyzed in terms of the possibilities that the environment presents to that particular organism. This move, says commentator Aaron Ben-Zeev, "transfers the main explanatory load from the animal's head to its environment. This requires . . . a very careful description of that environment." [25] To understand perception, Gibsonians suggest that we should "ask not what's inside your head, but what your head's inside of." [26] Details about habitats become as important to understanding perception as the details of the sensing organs of the organisms that dwell in them. This is not simply the obvious point that perception always takes place somewhere; it is the much more radical claim that the mechanics of the perceptual process must be understood in terms of a particular organism-environment engagement rather than simply in terms of optical laws. Understanding the nature of this textured landscape and the affordances it offers becomes an essential part of understanding perception. The environment is no longer just an object out onto which the sensory organs look. It is constitutive of the perceptual process. Philosopher of mind Mark Rowlands captures the radical nature of this proposal in his characterization of the Gibsonian view as making some of the very architecture of the perceiving mind *external* to perceiving the organism. [27]

From Perception to Cognition

The connection of perception and perceptual skills to the affordances of particular environments and to sensorimotor activities within those environments is further evidence that there are significant connections between place and mind. It appears that at least some of the activities of mind are not quite as contained in the head as had been traditionally assumed. But do Gibson's points about perception necessarily mean that cognition, too, is tied into the particularities of different physical environments just because perception is? Is knowing really as ecological as perceiving? This depends partly on just how close that connection hinted at by Plato between perceiving and knowing really is. Ecological psychologists think that the connection is very close indeed.

Even though he was a psychologist and not a philosopher, Gibson showed a fair amount of interest in the implications of his theory for epistemology. In a passage titled "A New Approach to Knowing," Gibson claimed that his theory "closes the supposed gap between perception and knowledge."[28] Both activities involve the abstraction of invariances from an array of environmental information. In the one case affordances are abstracted; in the other concepts are. Knowing is thereby merely an extension of perceiving. In the same passage, Gibson briefly tied his account of concepts into language. Language, he claimed, is simply a way of indicating certain affordances to members of the same species. Invariances are put into words to make explicit what had already been perceived. Not surprisingly, this happens at the cost of some loss of specificity. Words, according to Gibson, are severely limited relative to the breadth and complexity of what is actually picked up from the ambient array. He illustrated this with an example designed to poke fun at philosophers:

> Consider an adult, a philosopher, for example, who sees the cat on the mat. He knows that the cat is on the mat and believes the proposition and can say it, but all the time he plainly sees all sorts of wordless facts—the mat extending without interruption behind the cat, the far side of the cat, the cat hiding part of the mat, the edges of the cat, the cat being supported by the mat or resting on it, the horizontal rigidity of the floor under the mat and so on. The so-called concepts of extension of far and near, gravity, rigidity, horizontal, and so on, are nothing but partial abstractions from a rich but unitary perception of cat-on-mat. The parts of it he can name are called concepts, but they are not all of what he can see. (261)

Words convey descriptions of the invariances observed in the environment even though they can never capture the full extent of what the environment affords. But note where Gibson puts the main explanatory emphasis in this passage. The conceptual grasp of the cat being on the mat is located not in a proposition or a sentence held or spoken by the observer but in the observer's ability to pick up and identify the information present in the ambient array in the first place. The array bears the knowledge, and the observer picks it up directly.

Gibson did not take these epistemological thoughts very far, but he did insist that perception is just one among a number of similar modes of mental activity such as remembering, imagining, dreaming, desiring, expecting, and guessing. Like the enactivists, Gibson maintained not only that these mental activities are hard to distinguish in kind from each other but also that they are hard to distinguish in kind from sensorimotor activities.[29] Gibson's own speculations in this area are incomplete, and it was left to others who have followed him to fill them out.

Gibsonian Edward S. Reed made a systematic attempt to show how an ecological account of perception connects up with knowing. In *Encountering the*

World, Reed tied the ecological approach to perception first diachronically into an evolutionary story and then synchronically into an account of cognition. Reed did the former by suggesting that capacities for detecting information in the ambient array are selected by evolution. He did the latter by claiming that the central nervous system evolved not "as a commander of the body nor as a storehouse of ideas . . . [but] to maintain the animal's functional contact with its environment." [30] The evolution of consciousness effectively served to enable the organism to more efficiently make its way around the affordances offered by its surroundings. This position makes thought into "not an internal state of the mind or the brain but an ecological and functional state of an animal making its way through the environment" (67). Cognition becomes a process of making selections for how an organism is going to interact with information extant in the environment and not exclusively (or even principally) a matter of grasping propositions or following propositional rules. Psychology becomes the science of how animals place themselves into relations with environmental information. It is the study of a sensorimotor activity.

It is worth anticipating a popular objection at this point and noting that Reed's position is not a reduction of all knowledge to matters of "know how." Epistemologists typically deride know-how as being nothing more than the functional ability of an organism to achieve certain ends. These epistemologists take "knowing that," the grasping of the truth of propositions, to be the primary concern of their discipline. But it is simply not the case that ecological psychology reduces all knowing to know-how. Sensory knowledge is still very much about accurately recognizing what the environment affords and about being able to communicate this with others. It is not just a matter of finding the means to satisfy certain needs and desires. Gibson's hypothetical philosopher was expressing a truth, not just achieving a certain goal, when boldly announcing the presence of the feline on the rug. But although Gibsonians do not reduce perception and cognition to know-how, it is clear that recognizing and expressing the presence of an affordance is radically different from a mental light going on when something is cognitively grasped. Knowledge is a dynamic and ongoing process of an organism forging relationships to the possibilities presented by an environment and not the grasping of something held entirely in the head.

This ecological approach led Reed to characterize the study of cognition as "begin[ning] with an analysis of information and exploratory activity" (183). This information is located in the environment, and the exploratory activity is always something that an organism does in a particular place, niche, or biome. Knowing is primarily an activity that the organism does in the world rather than in its head. Reed adds that whatever cognitive skills an organism possesses are skills acquired in "specific cultural contexts; at particular places; within particular events and settings" (177). In light of this situatedness, Reed suggests that psychology should begin constructive dialogues with archeology, anthropology, and cultural geography. If Reed is right about this, then such a move would bring us into contact with the work of a number of the cultural naturalizers discussed in the previous chapter.

Gibsonians are not the only ones to elide the distinction between cognition and perception. Enactivists in cognitive science are eager to do the same thing. Varela, Thompson, and Rosch show how enactivism shares with ecological psychology the beliefs "that perception consists in perceptually guided action" and "that cognitive structures emerge from the recurrent sensori-motor patterns that enable action to be perceptually guided."[31] Cognition and perception, then, are both intimately connected to sensorimotor activity. They cite two important sets of experiments as evidence for these beliefs, the first of which connects perception to the sensorimotor activities of organisms in environments and the second of which makes the same connections for cognition.

The first experiment, performed in the 1950s, supports the hypothesis that perception is dependent upon being able to move around an environment.[32] Several kittens were raised in the dark. On the only occasions on which they were allowed access to light, half of the kittens were put in carriages, with each carriage being pulled by one of the remaining kittens. This arrangement ensured that pairs of kittens had very similar visual stimulations but, in each case, only one kitten was allowed to couple those stimuli with motor functions. When all the kittens were released from these constraints, the group that had towed the carriages around behaved normally. In contrast, the group of kittens that had been the passengers in the carriages bumped into objects and fell over ledges. It appeared that the group restricted to the carriages had literally not learned how to see because they had not been able to pair their visual experiences with action. The experiment suggests that the learning of perceptual skills is at some level connected to the learning of sensorimotor skills.

The second set of experiments makes the connection between sensorimotor action and cognition. These experiments, carried out by Eleanor Rosch and her research assistants, are about the formation of cognitive categories.[33] Grouping the world of appearances into distinct categories has always been seen as one of the most distinctive cognitive activities. Categorization explains why we usually characterize the things we sit on as chairs rather than as collections of molecules, pieces of wood, or cut-up trees. Rosch's experiments looked at the factors that determine the way categorizations occur. She discovered that the selection of categories is connected to embodied, sensorimotor action in an environment. Rosch's research revealed a basic level of categories established in such a way that it helps achieve optimal, functional interaction between organisms and their environments. It proved better for our survival, in other words, to categorize some flying things as birds rather than as collections of feathers or as indigo buntings. Darwin is at work again in ensuring that the basic level is arranged in such a way that it helps the organism to meet fundamental biological and cultural needs.

Rosch detailed several of the factors that influence the scale at which basic-level categorization occurs. One factor is directly concerned with how perception takes place. Basic-level categories usually occur at the level of those things that can be easily perceived by humans. Chairs and birds, for example, are such objects. Countries are not easily perceived, and neither are molecules. Another factor influencing the basic level is how the category functions in relation to the sensorimotor activity of the organism. Can an exemplar of the basic level be walked around, touched, picked up? Or would it require a view from thirty thousand feet to see the whole of it?

Rosch's account of basic-level categories makes it clear that biological constraints supplied by our bodies and by the way we interact with our environments play an important role in determining how we categorize. Since categorization is such an important part of cognition, these same embodied factors automatically become central to thought. Gibson had shared with Rosch the recognition that what counts as a thing in our world is connected to the facts of how we sense and move. He noted that it should be no surprise that "the size-level at which the environment exists is the intermediate one measured in millimeters and meters." [34] Gibson's position follows from his view that seeing is the rich activity of looking around, walking up to something, and viewing it from different angles. Gibsonians and enactivists share this important common ground. Both positions soften the boundary between perception and cognition by maintaining that both activities are integrally linked to facts about how animals move around their world. For dialectical biologists, the way that Gibsonians and enactivists connect perception and cognition to sensorimotor action in the environment should be particularly welcome. In dialectical biology, organisms create their world through their embodied activities. Organisms are not just the passive objects of extrinsic environmental stimuli. They are the modulators of those stimuli. The mutual enfolding of organism and environment appears to be a consistent feature of the biology, the psychology, and the cognitive science articulated in these three views.

Cognition and the Environment

Before the close of this chapter, there is one more technical and scientific location to discuss that moves us along the same path and adds weight to the general argument for the involvement of the environment in knowledge production. The situated movement in the philosophy of mind is a further indication that studies of thought and belief are increasingly broadening their sphere of interest beyond the brain and toward the engaged, materially embodied activities of organisms. A good example of this approach can be found in Mark Rowlands's environmentalist model of cognition.[35]

Rowlands distinguishes his environmentalist approach to mind from similar looking externalist approaches. Externalism in the philosophy of mind, associated with the work of Hilary Putnam, emerged out of the twin earth thought experiment.[36] In this thought experiment, we are asked to imagine a planet that duplicates ours in almost every respect—including the people that populate it—except that the liquid they call "water" on twin earth has a different chemical composition from the liquid we call "water" on this earth. Putnam pointed out that in light of this difference, even if every single other fact about this earth and about twin earth is identical, people on planet earth and people on twin earth cannot mean quite the same thing when they use the word "water." Even the identical brain states, down to the last neuronal firing, of persons on each of the twin earths is not enough to ensure that they both mean the same thing when they exclaim something like "I say, look at this water!" It cannot be enough because we know that they are talking about two different things. The lesson of the thought experiment is that meaning cannot depend entirely on what is going on inside the head. It must depend in part upon something external to the individual making the utterance. Putnam and his followers have named this view in the philosophy of mind "externalism" because it shows that some of what is needed to understand the meaning of an idea is external to the mind. Rowlands characterizes the view as semantic externalism because it is mental states with semantic content—states such as believing, desiring, and thinking—that are shown to depend on facts about the external world to get their meaning.

Now this might sound like a rather basic observation, but it actually has a dramatic implication for certain views of mind. For example, it vigorously challenges Descartes's complete separation of the mental and the physical by denying that the contents of the mind are meaningful when they are alienated from facts that lie outside in the physical world. The kind of introspective methodology that Descartes employed in his *Mediations* for understanding the world becomes completely inadequate. Externalism shows that there is much about the world that Descartes could not possibly understand if he went about manufacturing knowledge from completely inside his head. Semantic externalism is dramatic because it gives us minds that are never completely self-contained. Rowlands claims that it presents to us the realization that "the mind is penetrated by the world."[37]

But even if it offers a substantial challenge to some of the traditional pictures, Rowlands believes that semantic externalism does not go far enough. Not only does semantic externalism fail to have anything important to say about nonsemantic mental processes—processes such as perceiving, remembering information, and reasoning—but it also fails to externalize enough of the actual workings of the mind. It makes neither the architecture nor the process of cognition in any way external to the head. The environmentalist view of mind that Rowlands advocates in its place takes this extra step. It describes a mind some of whose reasoning structures are literally located outside the head and in the world. It is not just the content of the mind that depends on the world; some of its very architecture does, too.

The arguments that Rowlands employs to make his case for the environmentalist model of the mind fill a whole book in their own right, and this is not the place to repeat them. But he does look for support in some familiar arenas. For example, he includes arguments from evolutionary biology to show how the utilization of external structures in cognitive process is likely to have been naturally selected. He explains how Gibson's optic array can be thought of as an external structure that an organism manipulates and transforms during the sensorimotor part of the perceptual process, suggesting that this makes certain aspects of perception external to the head. And he describes physical reminders such as knots tied in fabric and distinctive books on library shelves as environmental structures that secure at least some of our information-processing load in the world rather than in the head. It is not just that the content of a belief is found in the world as in semantic externalism; in many cases the actual processing of that information also goes on in the world external to the cognizing body. He refers to this stronger view as "psychotectonic externalism."[38] Unlike semantic externalism, the mind is not just penetrated by the world, but a good portion of the mind is literally in the world.

Rowlands's arguments for the externality of at least some of our cognitive architecture are given inductive support by recent trends in research into artificial intelligence. It is now generally recognized that promising early research in artificial intelligence and robotics failed to bear the fruit that once appeared likely. When robots were designed to achieve tasks in the world by creating an internal representation of their environment and then reasoning centrally according to the formal manipulation of rules, the robots failed spectacularly to achieve even relatively simple tasks. It began to seem that R2D2-like entities delivering the coffee were about as much as artificial intelligence could manage.

Andy Clark has described the much greater successes of a robot named Herbert who, when set the task of entering a room and picking up aluminum cans, goes about things in a quite different way. Herbert does not scan the room for the cans and form a complex and integrated plan of how to pick up each can based on that initial input. Rather, he puts to use "a collection of coarse sensors and simple [and] relatively independent behavioral routines" to achieve the same end.[39] Herbert moves randomly though the room and stops only if vaguely tablelike objects appear directly in front of him. He then reaches out and sweeps a robotic arm across the table surface only if he manages to center a canlike object in his field of vision, and he clasps his robotic fingers together only when such a sweep succeeds in bumping against something solid. Rather than having a single, complex program that has to solve the identification, locomotion, and collection problems all in one go, Herbert is a much simpler kind of creature all together. There are a few basic things that he can do, and then he uses constant feedback from his environment—feedback basically in the form of bumping into things—to incrementally zero in on the cans and to successfully collect them. He solves the problem of picking up the cans not because he possesses a highly sophisticated central processing system but because he has cleverly integrated sensorimotor and perceptual systems along with the mastery of just enough embodied patterns of behavior. Despite being a relatively simple robot, Herbert is remarkably adept at his tasks. His success is a product of a "layered cognitive architecture" that has the world and his body acting in concert with his mind. This mind needs only as much sophistication as is necessary to keep his body in functional contact with its environment. Clark describes the lesson drawn from Herbert to be "an increasing awareness of the important interpenetration . . . of perception, thought, and action."[40] Research programs like Clark's investigate what is now commonly known as the "extended mind."

In *Being There: Putting Brain, Body, and World Together Again*, Clark makes a comprehensive case for rejecting approaches to artificial intelligence that begin with the algorithmic manipulation of symbolic representations of the world. In its place, he interprets the lessons learned from such devices as Herbert to be that intelligence is primarily a means of engaging with the world. This engagement involves extending the mind through the use of "active strategies that leave much of the information out in the world, and cannily using iterated, real-time sequences of body-world interactions to solve problems in a robust and flexible way" (98). Clark concludes that these directions in robotics and artificial intelligence in turn demand a reconception of how we regard human intelligence. He asks that we "abandon the image of ourselves as essentially disembodied reasoning engines . . . and of environment as simply a source of problem-specifying inputs and an arena for action" (273). Once this view has been rejected—a view that bears all the hallmarks of the Platonist, modernist, cognitivist, and adaptationist themes we have criticized—it must be replaced with one of brain, body, and world dynamically engaging with each other in the rich interaction with the earth that we have come to know as cognition. The extended mind is firmly grounded in its physical environment. It singularly fails to transcend it.

THE DIFFERENT TEXTURES OF ENVIRONMENTS

This direction in the philosophy of mind and in cognitive science, although radical enough within that tradition, is merely the latest and most focused reincarnation of a set of claims that has appeared sporadically across a range of disciplines over the last fifty years. In 1967, for example, Eric H. Lenneberg suggested in *The Biological Foundations of Language* that the categories used in language were based on prototypes supplied by the external environment. Edith Cobb posited a connection between cognition and landscape in *The Ecology of Imagination in Childhood* (1977). Cobb claimed that the process of childhood play in nature supplied a context that enabled children to structure their relations to human others. In *The Savage Mind* (1966), Claude Lévi-Strauss offered a theory about a fundamental homology between the systems of differentiation used in primal societies in their relations with each other and the systems of differentiation that these societies found in contacts with their ecological environment. Another of Paul Shepard's provocative essays described lyrically how our ancestors "assembled the self cognitively by reference to extensive fauna swallowed bit by bit."[41] In recent times, a whole new field known as "ecopsychology" has emerged in response to Shepard's worry about the loss of these historic possibilities in contemporary life.[42]

When the contemporary scientific work described in this chapter is placed atop these older ideas, this combined evidence suggests that we should be paying more attention to the structural importance of the physical environments in which people act in order to fully understand the process of thought. Ignoring the relevance of the physical environment significantly hinders our ability to understand ourselves and our beliefs. Environments play a significant constitutive role in thought.

This claim about physical environments calls for an important cautionary note. Environments should always be considered in their broadest possible sense so that they include *both* cultural *and* material factors. Enactivist Mark Johnson makes it clear that environment includes "our history, culture, language, institutions, theories, and so forth."[43] Cultural and physical environments are never entirely separable. Feminist standpoint theorists have shown that oppressive social environments can actually end up exerting a wide range of physical forces upon the bodies of those who are forced to work and make their homes in such environments. But to repeat Pickering's point discussed in chapter 2, it is important that the discussion of social environments not be allowed to eclipse the less recognized but significant influence of physical environments. Postmodern epistemologies have typically prioritized cultural over material factors. An adequate account of knowing must be one that reveals the significance of our physical engagement with the places in which we dwell.

Once we are prepared to accept that physical environments are epistemically relevant, we need to remember that these places are not simply homogeneous spaces in which movement, perception, and cognitive interaction can occur. It is precisely the heterogeneity of places that provides the distinctive interactions that give shape to our embodied minds in the first place. If the earth were a perfectly smooth sphere, our perceptual and cognitive lives would doubtless be significantly poorer. Different physical environments, both natural and artificial, supply radically different experiences for those who move about them. These differences are likely to have cognitive significance. An aqueous environment provides different balance and energy requirements from a terrestrial one. Life in a village on the steep slopes of a Himalayan mountain affords different physical challenges from life in Manhattan, and both these environments in turn provide radically different experiences from those afforded to fishermen off the Aleutian Islands of southwestern Alaska. Laboratory studies theorists such as Ed Hutchins, Bruno Latour, Karin Knorr-Cetina, and Andrew Pickering are already treating the gritty details of those diverse physical environments as epistemically relevant. Outside of laboratories, we should begin to consider as cognitively significant the full range of experiences that the earth's richly textured landscapes afford.

Johnson admits in the middle of his enactivist account of cognition that the physical environment is "structured in ways that limit the possibilities for our categorizations of it."[44] Environments do not supply endless possibilities for all organisms but provide specific limits based on the kinds of opportunities afforded to particular organisms. Humans cannot jump off tall buildings and expect to fly, and city dwellers can rarely expect the silence necessary for listening to the birds. Residents of extreme northern and southern latitudes cannot expect consistent periods of daylight throughout the year, and those living in arid regions must always make provision against the possibility of a crop-threatening drought. There is not an infinite amount of cognitive structuring potential out there. In addition to these purely physical limitations provided by the environment, different facets of social organization also restrict the kinds of physical engagement that it is practical for people to have with any given environment. Certain cities do not provide safe environments for walking late at night, and most of us who are used to eating out of grocery stores would find living off the land nearly impossible wherever we tried it. The environmental experiences that structure cognition will be different depending upon where the agent of knowledge is located, what practices the agent engages in, and what cultural values the agent possesses.

If the structures of the physical environment do indeed supply some limiting factors for our categorizations, then environments should not be treated as valueless generic spaces that merely supply organisms with a space for thinking. They should be considered highly particularized microenvironments that afford different possibilities to different organisms. The physical environment is not just a homogeneous space in which knowing happens to occur, but a highly particularized and value-laden place continually presenting possibilities for embodied engagement. Incorporating this insight into epistemology means moving away from treating the physical environment as a mere "site" for human activity, as Edward Casey has put the received view.[45] Environments should be regarded as having significantly different characters that make important contributions to how we know. As a result, the student of cognition must heed Ed Hutchins's advice and articulate the relevant details of physical environments "rich in organizing resources."

I am fascinated by what Samuel sees and what I
am missing. In the Great Basin I can read the
landscape well. I know the subtleties of place. A
horned lizard buried in the sand cannot miss my
eyes because I anticipate his. A kit fox at night
streaks across the road. His identity is told by the
beam of my headlights. And when a great
horned owl hoots above my head, I hoot too.
Home is the range of one's instincts.

Terry Tempest Williams, *An Unspoken Hunger*

4   Active Landscapes

David Abram has described the enveloping earth as "the
very ground and horizon of all our knowing."[1] It had always been clear that
the earth provided the ground and horizon for all our embodied experience.
Abram's comment eloquently reminds us that this same earth also grounds all
our cognitive experiences. On the basis of the evidence presented in chapters
2 and 3 about the connections between the place and mind, we might begin to
agree with Abram and to view with suspicion the ancient and modern credos
that reason enables humans to transcend all aspects of our physical location
and obtain knowledge as if disengaged from the body and the earth—a view
from nowhere.

Humans are in the strange, and maybe unique, position of simultaneously
being products of the earth, formed and propelled through time by evolutionary forces, and creatures with the capacity to look back at the earth and tell
stories about how we think it functions. We are part of earth's story, and earth
is part of ours. It was forgetting the former that created the illusion of a view
from nowhere in the latter. Letting the participation of the earth quietly slip
from the picture came at the cost of allowing what is really a dialogue between

mind and world to transform itself into an arrogant monologue, or even into an inquisition. Francis Bacon was guilty of this mistake (and of adding several layers of gendered oppression to boot) when he described natural science as a process of "wresting nature's secrets from her" in order to continue "the propogat[ion] of man's empire over the universe."[2] A particular view of epistemology in the hands of people such as Bacon was just one piece of an emergent modern worldview that created an exploitative attitude toward the earth. We might reasonably suspect that Abram's different view of epistemology is an important component of a worldview that promotes a more generous and benign attitude toward the earth.

Philosophers have certainly worked hard to sustain the old view. From Socrates' debates with Theaetetus to Descartes's retreat into his stove-heated room right up to the arrival of naturalized epistemologies in the second half of the twentieth century, the study of the production of knowledge in the dominant tradition of Western philosophy has been pursued in settings designed to maintain the illusion that knowing is about transcending one's natural situation in order to know from nowhere. The library and the closed office space have usually been considered the most reliable sites for the production of philosophical knowledge. The freedom from sensory distraction that these places offer allows philosophers to forget for a while that they are embodied creatures and enables them to engage in what appears to be the purest of all kinds of work, the work of the mind. In these settings, the enveloping earth is nowhere in sight. The idea that the study of knowledge might be pursued empirically by watching how scientists behave or scientifically by testing how cognition actually functions in the thick of things is often still scoffed at by theorists of knowledge eager to prop up ideas about the nobility and purity of their quest.[3]

If the evidence presented so far is to be believed, it is time to change all this. Dialectical biology, ecological studies of perception, enactivist cognitive science, and environmentalist approaches to the philosophy of mind all provide evidence that the project of richly naturalizing epistemology means looking at how the particular spaces and places in which we do our thinking contribute to the knowledge we create. "Place" is recognized here for the first time as a technical term. Places have a relevant particularity and character that simple geometrical spaces lack.[4] Not only are they made up of the physical realities of mountains and savannahs, cities and oceans, but they are also drenched in cultural meaning. Yi-Fu Tuan, the cultural geographer who coined the distinction between space and place, calls places "centers of cultural value."[5] Space is something abstract and undifferentiated that is simply moved through or mapped from the outside. Places are the result of people pausing for a while in a location and instilling some of their cultural values into the landscape. The approaches described in the last chapter are more likely to claim that it is space that counts cognitively. The natural sciences are usually eager to describe environments that are free of cultural values. But the previously mentioned tension between cultural and scientific forms of naturalizing surfaces again briefly here. The fact that, even as scientists, we move through laboratory spaces according to different cultural practices and roles means that it must also be place, not just space, that actively participates in cognition. The environmental structures that filter into cognition seem like they must include both physical and cultural components.

The current chapter is written with this in mind. It offers some new areas of support for the idea that environments are active participants in the process out of which knowledge is constructed. This chapter moves away from evidence in the hard sciences and toward cultural geography, anthropology, and personal narrative to support the connection between place and mind. The move to these different kinds of sources is strategic. Just as there were pragmatic reasons to present some arguments exclusively from the science side of the divide, so are there reasons to present some arguments exclusively from the cultural side. Stepping away from the natural sciences creates a number of particularly valuable rhetorical openings through which to work an argument such as mine. One opening is that it provides a way to talk for the first time about the environmentally potent idea of a "sense of place." Senses of place are hard to discuss in a scientific context because people in these disciplines are actively—though often vainly—trying to eliminate all the traces of cultural values from their accounts. Outside of scientific discourse, places in all their rich cultural and physical particularity are more often allowed to wash over those seeking a standpoint from which to make claims about the earth. If work in the natural sciences is needed to remedy something Andy Pickering called the neglect of the material, then it might take work in areas that make fewer claims to scientific purity to remedy the neglect of a sense of place.

Another characteristic that distinguishes this chapter from the last is that it pays more attention to knowledge created in natural rather than in artificial environments. I acknowledge that the distinction between what is natural and what is artificial is a slippery one. Everything that humans do obeys the laws of nature and so must be natural to some degree. The nature/artifice distinction also appears to be one of those constructs that have worked harmfully to sever humans from nature rather than to integrate them into it. But slippery and problematic though it may be, it is still possible to hold onto a useful distinction between the natural and the artificial, between such environments as the inside of an automobile and the inside of a temperate rainforest. In fact, without some form of the nature/artifice distinction still operating, it is hard to imagine reasons for environmentalists to seek the preservation of the former rather than the latter. The distinction is useful in this chapter to differentiate such environments as cities and laboratories, which are composed of mostly manufactured objects put in those arrangements by humans, from such environments as old-growth forests and floodplains, which have come to their present states through processes that for the most part have not involved humans.[6] Thus the places discussed in this chapter are not laboratories but glacial outwash plains, not neurocircuits in the brain but arid hillsides and valleys peopled with creekside cottonwood trees.

Turning the focus to natural environments is also important for the trajectory of the book. One of my main goals is to take a fairly technical point in epistemology and to show that it has relevance to environmental philosophy. Given that environmental philosophy is most often about natural environments, connecting place and mind in the scientific laboratory might appear to be of only passing interest to the environmental philosopher. In laboratory studies, the kinds of environments shown to be epistemically relevant are highly contrived, artificial environments of lasers, spectrometers, and deflection devices. In chapter 2, I suggest that it is possible to take the basic science studies insight outside the lab. Showing now that the same story has application to a range of natural environments is important if the environmental philosopher is to begin to take note. Shepard spoke of minds operating "in a surround of living plants, rich in texture, smell, and motion." It is this kind of surround that the environmental philosopher is eager to find reasons to protect.

Previous chapters call upon figures not typically associated with the Western epistemological tradition to make this case, and the discussion in this chapter ventures even further away from the tradition. But first, it is worth taking a moment to note briefly how the idea that place should be taken seriously is not entirely alien to the Western philosophical tradition. One of the few contemporary writers to have systematically discussed the significance of place in Western philosophy, Edward S. Casey, titled one of his books *Getting Back into Place*, suggesting that Western philosophy was once into place. Despite the fact that I characterize the roots of the problematic view that distances us from the physical realities of our environment as Platonic, Casey shows that things are not quite as straightforward as that. There was the odd moment when even Plato showed some sensitivity to the view that places are epistemically involved in the claims that we make.

PLATO AND LANDSCAPE

In the *Timaeus,* Plato told a story about origins that grappled with the question of what existed before the created world. The coming-to-be of the world, Plato reasoned, must occur in some place since nothing can come to be in no place. Plato posited a certain kind of space, which he called *chora,* as the location in which the sensory world was generated. *Chora,* he said, provided "a home for all created things."[7] It was the original space. When the Demiurge created the world and the objects that populated it, he set them all within this *chora.*

Chora occupies a position of considerable significance in Plato's account of cosmogenesis. Only the divine craftsman, the models (forms) he used, and *chora* existed prior to the coming into being of the physical world. The status of time was secondary to that of place, since time was bestowed on nature only after creation, apparently so that the Demiurge might have a "moving image of eternity" (37d). Of *chora*'s exact nature, Plato claimed that we have only a "dreamlike sense" (52c). But we know enough about it to say that it was a rather curious kind of entity. *Chora* itself, existing prior to the creation of any object, was less of a thing than a receiving principle. But it must also have existed in some physical sense if it were to have provided a place in which things could have been received. Plato often used the term for a "receptacle" when he spoke about *chora.* The status of *chora* was thus unusual and a bit ambiguous. It was not quite material itself, but it must have had something substantial to it if it were to have been a receptacle for material things.

The interesting thing about *chora* is that it turns out to have been not entirely passive when acting as this receptacle for created things. For part of the time, Plato portrayed *chora* as if it were an amorphous piece of clay that simply took up the shape of the world when imprinted with the forms that the divine craftsman used as his model. "She is the natural recipient of all impressions and is stirred and informed by them" (50b–c), Plato announced. This initially looks like only a passive role for *chora,* but *chora* also had an influence on the shapes that were taken up. As well as being a receptacle for created things, *chora*'s ambiguous status allowed it to also *condition* the things that were created. *Chora* was the "nurse of generation" that, with the help of the Demiurge, formed *out of her own being* the rich spectrum of individual entities that populate creation. *Chora* possessed some resilience around which the crafts-man had to work when he created the "strange variety of appearances" (52d) contained in the sensible world. Plato's *chora*, which he described as "full of powers" (52d), clearly exerted a subtle influence over what came into being.

Since the *Timaeus* was not just a story about the generation of the world but also a story about how that world came to be comprehensible to us, these remarks about *chora's* potency have considerable relevance to epistemology. This becomes clear in Plato's explanation of how the sensible world came to be intelligible. Plato explained how "out of disorder [the Demiurge] brought order, considering that this was in every way better than the other" (30a). This order was a product of both the *logos* brought in through the forms that were the models for creation and of the necessity that was already there in *chora*. Casey characterized these two factors that make the world intelligible as a pair of triangles (one upright, one inverted) touching at their tips. He claimed that "the bottom triangle represents the 'abyss' and 'turbulent welter' of the Receptacle . . . and the upper triangle the 'order and design' of mathemati-cal rationality."[8] Creation occurred at the point at which the two triangles touched. The disorder of *chora* was tempered by the rational order of *logos* to produce the objects of the sensible world. The world of sense experience became intelligible only as a result of a pair of influences: one the uncreated and indestructible realm of the forms, a realm of pure reason (*logos*), and the other the materiality of the receptacle (*chora*) acting as the nurse of generation when these forms are imprinted on it. The intelligibility of the sensed world is indebted to both of these influences.

Plato clearly acknowledged a certain kind of potency to *chora* that is relevant to matters of thought and mind. *Chora* adopts both an active and a passive role in creating appearances when it "receives all things and in some mysterious way partakes of the intelligible" (51b). But the skeptic might reasonably inquire whether there is any evidence that the alleged epistemic potency of *chora* was ever transferred from the rather abstract discussion of cosmology and creation in the *Timaeus* to anything more particular and concrete in Plato's other di-alogues. *Chora* may matter in the *Timaeus*, but did Plato really show that he cared about actual places anywhere else? There is at least one dialogue that contains some intriguing hints that he did.

In the *Phaedrus*, Plato suggested several times that the particular place from which Socrates spoke might have lent shape to the kinds of things he said. When Phaedrus led Socrates outside of the city with the promise of Lysias's speech, Socrates appeared to appreciate that the place in which they settled would subtly influence their discussion. Though Socrates was wont to claim that the countryside had nothing to teach him, this time, on arrival at their chosen spot, he waxed eloquent about the beauty of the place. Sounding more like John Muir having a High Sierra moment than the committed urbanite that he was, Socrates rhapsodized:

> it really is a beautiful resting place. The plane tree is tall and very broad; the chaste-tree, high as it is, is wonderfully shady, and since it is in full bloom, the whole place is filled with its fragrance. From under the plane tree the loveliest spring runs with very cool water—our feet can testify to that. The place appears to be dedicated to Achelous and some of the Nymphs, if we can judge from the statues and votive offerings. Feel the freshness of the air; how pretty and pleasant it is; how it echoes with the summery, sweet song of the cicadas' chorus! The most exquisite thing of all, of course, is the grassy slope: it rises so gently that you can rest your head perfectly when you lie down on it. You have really been the most marvelous guide, my dear Phaedrus. (230b–c)[9]

Socrates felt so inspired by his location that he began his speech by confessing to Phaedrus that he was "in the grip of something divine" and "on the edge of speaking in dithyrambs" (238c). The place elevated Socrates in some surprising way. Phaedrus, for his part, remarked that Socrates appeared to be "totally out of place" and that his speech contained "an unusual flow of words" relative to Socrates' norm (230c).

In the dialogue that followed, Socrates was uncharacteristically dismissive of Lysias's speech and uncharacteristically confident about his own ability as a rhetorician. "I wouldn't even think that Lysias himself could be proud of it," said Socrates when Phaedrus finished reading the transcript of Lysias's speech. He then added confidently, "my breast is full and I feel that I can make a different speech, . . . better than Lysias'" (235a,c). When he began speaking, Socrates outlined his theory of the forms to Phaedrus, but with some important amendments and additions that were articulated here for the first time. In the myth he tells about the two-horse chariot, Socrates added detail to his suggestion in the *Meno* that knowledge of the forms is a matter of remembering something known from an earlier life. Given that Plato is all along hinting that the unusual outside setting contributed something extra to Socrates' thought, it hardly seems an accident that the theory of the forms began to change as a result of the change of place. "There's something really divine about this place," Socrates told Phaedrus. "Don't be surprised if I'm quite taken by the Nymphs' madness as I go on with the speech" (238d). Going outside of the city and into a very unusual location in nature clearly had an effect on Socrates. Two of Plato's commentators, Alexander Nehemas and Paul

Woodruff, characterize this peculiar aspect of the *Phaedrus* as follows: "The countryside for which Socrates has left Athens, has turned him, surprisingly, into an accomplished rhetorician. Much more surprisingly, however, it has provided him with an opportunity to cast doubt on views that, within the fiction of Plato's dialogues, he had developed within the city walls. This Odysseus returns home from abroad a different man indeed."[10] Even for Plato, places, on occasion, appear to count.

Though one can perhaps identify the odd passage in which the physical environment seemed to be given considerable epistemic significance by Plato, these passages are few and far between. The general direction of Platonic thought was away from the importance to knowledge of material situation and toward a conception of knowledge as abstract, disembodied, and unplaced. The history outlining the gradual decline in the significance of place that began with Plato has been well told by Casey.[11] There is no need to tell any more of that story here, except to report that Casey's detailed account traces what he calls "the gradual and forceful encroachment of space upon place."[12] The potency of actual places was systematically eclipsed by the conception of inert and impotent geometrical spaces. As a result of this encroachment, anything philosophically relevant about the particularity of places was effaced by the homogeneity of space, understood as simply infinite extension by Descartes and as absolute geometrical space by Newton. Geographers have referred to this encroachment as the gradual "evacuation" of place in Western thought. Location in absolute space became merely incidental to the study of more philosophically interesting things such as propositions, actions, or events. In Casey's terms, places were reconfigured into "sites" that lacked any kind of relevance to matters of thought and mind. But once outside this Western philosophical tradition, you do not have to go far to find ways of thinking in which places have never been evacuated of their significance.

Indigenous North American Relations to Place

If it is the case that places come to exert a subtle influence on how we know, then this influence will likely be most evident in communities that have lived in the same places for long periods of time. Indigenous cultures have long been perceived as having a connection to the land that immigrant cultures lack. Nonnomadic groups of indigenous peoples can often claim to have lived in and around the same places continuously for centuries. Ever since Diamond Jenness's ethnographies of the Ojibwa peoples in the 1930s, researchers have studied Native American cultures to learn about their social, ethical, and religious relationships to the lands in which they live.[13] Because these relationships often involve respect for the nonhuman communities that share these lands, professional environmental ethicists have subsequently championed indigenous peoples as exemplars of how to be in the right kind of moral relationship with the land.[14] Much of this academic scrutiny has been unwelcome. Vine Deloria Jr. has written that every culture has a curse, and that the particular curse of Indian culture is anthropology.[15] Native Americans have rightfully lamented the careless generalizations across diverse traditions that have been made, the lack of apparent interest in the current situation of indigenous North American peoples, and the selective appropriation of only those parts of an indigenous belief system that anthropologists or environmental ethicists think they can use.[16]

In light of these criticisms, the remarks on the next few pages are made with some trepidation.[17] Perhaps it is helpful to remember that the intention here is not to champion any one particular set of moral or religious beliefs over any other. The remarks are presented as another piece of the evidence to create the broadest possible case in support of a particular view of how places can influence belief. Unlike some of the discussion of Native American belief practices in environmental ethics, this should not be read as a plea for a kind of conversion to a better way of life. The purpose is only to examine how the relationship between thought and environment operates in the knowledge practices of a group that has lived in the same place for a long period of time. This group could have been any group that has lived continuously in one area and has turned that space into a textured place, brimming over with cultural meaning.

Keith Basso has told an intriguing story of how one physical environment has become integrated into a belief system by a culture long resident in a particular place.[18] Basso spent twenty-two years living and studying among the Western Apache in Cibecue, Arizona. During his time with the Western Apache, Basso learned from a cattleman named Dudley Patterson that particular places on tribal lands could be used for moral guidance. Patterson told Basso how the Western Apache rely on places in order to teach them the smoothness, the resilience, and the steadiness of mind necessary to live rightly. Some of these morally powerful places are the sites in which Western Apache ancestors were buried. This means that a certain amount of moral insight is gained from practicing the respect demanded by the presence of the ancestors resting there. But the wisdom that the places provide appears to come not simply from the bones of the ancestors but also from other aspects of the places concerned. In particular, some of this wisdom emerges from the ongoing role that the land plays in the cultural experiences of the Western Apache.

Basso first became aware of this role when he heard Patterson say quietly to a fellow cattle hand who had missed several days of work, "Trail Goes Down Between Two Hills will make you wise" (114). Basso learned that the stories associated with particular places, in this case a story about two beautiful sisters teasing Old Man Owl at a place where a trail runs between two hills, could be used to give indirect criticism or advice to a person when a direct approach was inappropriate. Once a person knew a particular place and the story associated with it, merely reciting the name given by the Western Apache to the place could conjure up the particular moral wisdom it carried. When the cultural narrative was set atop the physical geography of the landform—in other words, when the place had been made through its appearance in a story—the land became an agent with a specific role to play in the moral life of the people living there. After having been told the story of Trail Goes Down Between Two Hills by Patterson, Basso remarked on how the narrative had "transformed its referent from a geographical site into something resembling a theater, a natural stage upon the land . . . where significant moral dramas unfolded in the past" (121). Basso determined to research what Patterson had told him a bit further.

At the beginning of his study, in order to clarify the nature of his research, Basso asked Patterson, "what is wisdom?" Patterson responded not with a definition but with a statement about where to find it: "[I]t's in these places. Wisdom sits in places" (121). Patterson responded to Basso's further inquiry about how to become wise with the following remarks: "How will you walk along this trail of wisdom? Well, you will go to many places. You must look at them closely. You must remember all of them. Your relatives will talk to you about them. You must remember everything they tell you. You must think about it and keep on thinking about it, and keep on thinking about it. You must do this because no one can help you but yourself. If you do this, your mind will become smooth. It will become steady and resilient. You will walk a long way and live a long time" (126). Patterson added that just as one needs to drink water to stay alive, so one needs to drink wisdom from places in order to become wise.

Basso confessed a certain amount of confusion about the language Patterson had used to express the process of becoming wise. He had not received anything like the definition of wisdom he had expected. The idea of drinking from places was completely alien to him. He was baffled by what he called the "covert cultural logic" to which he was not a party. But it was significant that

Patterson did not leave Basso to figure out these metaphors by himself in his head. This was not the kind of wisdom that could be grasped purely cognitively. Patterson actually took Basso out on horseback to these different places so that Basso could experience the places with his body as Patterson taught him their names and told him what had happened at each place a long time ago. This education, carried out over many long, hot days on horseback, was designed to achieve a state in which the mere mention of a name would evoke as much as possible about both the particular physical location and the experience of being there. Only then could the name be used to evoke a particular piece of practical wisdom about how to live rightly.

The fact that Basso had to feel the character of these places in person in order to know what they taught makes it clear that it is not simply the telling of the story that generates the wisdom. If it were, then the places themselves would have only a symbolic role, reminding the Western Apache of culturally constructed accounts. Instead, in order to drink wisdom from its repository in these places, Basso had to know the places for himself. The topography of the land had to filter through his limbs, the smell of the vegetation had to permeate his clothes, and the sweat created by the struggle of getting there had to drip from his body onto the ground. Only after the land had made this contact with his body and had left its imprint there could the story about what happened long ago at a place like Trail Goes Down Between Two Hills begin to reveal its full meaning.

David Abram calls the kind of experience that Patterson was trying to convey to Basso when he took him to these places a "synaesthetic participation" with the animate surroundings.[19] With synaesthetic *participation* (as opposed to just synaesthetic *perception*), mountains, canyons, and streams present themselves to the senses with an "expressive potency and dynamism." This kind of participation, claims Abram, is more often found in oral than in literate cultures. "A particular place in the land," he continues, "is never, for an oral culture, just a passive or inert setting for the human events that occur there. It is an active participant in these occurrences. Indeed by virtue of its underlying and enveloping presence the place may even be felt to be the source, the primary power that expresses itself through the various events that unfold there."[20] The hidden potency of the places is hinted at by one of Basso's collaborators, who said to him, "the land is always stalking people."[21]

Basso concluded that the sense of place of the Western Apache, or the "sensing of place," as he preferred to call it, is part of the activity that creates Apache cultural and moral identity. He called it the sensing of place because it is the ongoing, synaesthetic interaction of a people with their physical environment that creates the attachment, not an idea grasped by a disembodied intellect. Unlike most of those who discuss a sense of place, Basso is reluctant to characterize this Western Apache sensing of place in any mystical terms, calling it instead "a commonplace occurrence . . . an ordinary way of engaging one's surroundings and finding them significant."[22] It is something that the Western Apache simply do in their day-to-day lives. A sensing of place is not a vague feeling of attachment but an ongoing dynamic interaction between a people and their world. It is not about warm feelings of nostalgia but about animacy. Basso makes clear the agency of particular places in the knowledge systems of the Western Apache when he notes how the people "show by their actions that their surroundings live in them" (146). The places are more than just sites in which actions and events happen to occur; they are personalities that are engaging with human actors at every moment.

The moral knowledge carried by the particular places that Dudley Patterson tried to explain to Keith Basso was clearly not spoken entirely by the places themselves. It was a product of the culture having lived and died in those geographies over many generations. Basso notes how the knowledge or wisdom that the places supply is learned from "observing different places (thus to recall them quickly and clearly), learning their Apache names (thus to identify them in spoken discourse and song), and reflecting on traditional narratives that underscore the virtues of wisdom" (134). But despite the obvious importance of the cultural narrative for making these places significant, it would be wrong to suggest that all of the significance of the place is the product of the Western Apache people. It is important to resist overemphasizing the cultural factors. The character of the places is also at work determining the kind of narrative that can be told at each place. It is the topography and aridity of the land at Trail Goes Down Between Two Hills that made it possible for Two Sisters to tease Old Man Owl for his lasciviousness. Trail Goes Down Between Two Hills has a character that lends itself only to a certain kind of story. The rich sense of place that the Western Apache have created around Cibecue is a blend of personal, cultural, and natural factors. Basso describes it as consisting of "a stream of symbolically drawn particulars—the visible particulars of local topographies, the personal particulars of biographical associations, and the notional particulars of socially given systems of thought" (144). The material, personal, and social components are all at work. It is what Basso calls "a kind of imaginative experience, a species of involvement with the natural and social environment" (143). The complexity of the relationship between the natural and cultural factors wafts continually through Basso's account.

Vine Deloria Jr. describes a similar, and perhaps even stronger, role for the natural and material factors in his generalized account of Native American religious belief.[23] Deloria juxtaposes what he characterizes as a Native approach to religion with a Christian approach in order to illustrate their respective emphases on space and time. He chastises Western European Christians for never having learned "to consider the nature of the world from a spatial point of view" (63). Deloria argues that the sequence of events described in the Bible from creation through to the crucifixion encourages Christians to focus on time instead of place. "The very essence of western European identity," claims Deloria, "involves the assumption that time proceeds in a linear fashion" (63). The notion of manifest destiny as the unfolding of events according a divine plan adds the belief that the line represents moral progress. The expansion westward across the North American continent by Christian European immigrants and the taming of the wilderness that they found there could then be interpreted as examples of staying on course. Deloria faults Western European Christians for acting as if "the torch of enlightenment was fated to march from the Mediterranean to the San Francisco Bay" (69). This failure to consider the world from a spatial point of view is connected, claims Deloria, to Christianity's wanton neglect of the natural environment.

Deloria explains some striking contrasts between these Christian approaches and the religious beliefs of American Indians. He insists that history is less important for Native Americans since "the structure of religious traditions is taken directly from the world around them" (66). "Value judgments," says Deloria, "involve present community realities and not a reliance on the part of future golden ages toward which the community is moving or from which the community has veered" (68). Religious experience is valued primarily for what it can teach people about how to live in a particular place today. Religious revelation is seen as "a continuous process of adjustment to the natural surroundings and not as a specific message valid for all times and places" (67). The structure of religious belief is therefore found not in some transcendent, abstract realm but in actual lived relationships with landscapes and other forms of life.

The emphasis on learning how to live right in a place means that it is not so important to learn an accurate chronology of events in order to understand a tribal religion. Deloria tells how the recounting of tribal histories is usually prefaced with a casual "the way I heard it" or "it was a long time ago." The recording of history becomes always an approximate affair with precision demanded only for the interpretation of why those events took place. The date of a migration, for example, is always less important than the reason why the people had to move. Tribes typically combine history with geography to produce a sacred geography, one that stores historical events in stories associated with particular places on tribal lands. An effective way of learning a tribal history is to be guided around this sacred geography by a tribal elder. In a sacred geography, history is told—as it was told to Keith Basso by Dudley Patterson—in terms of what happened *here* instead of what happened *then*. "Spatial thinking," Deloria suggests, "requires that ethical systems be related directly to the physical world and real human situations" (73). Tribal religious and moral knowledge is, for this reason, always a geographically situated and practical knowledge.

Elements of the complex relationship between the personal, the social, and the physical that emerged in Basso's account of moral practices are also evident in Deloria's more generalized account of Native religion. Narratives about culturally important events at particular places take on a key role in the formation of religious belief. The land becomes imbued with meaning through the history of a tribe's residence there. But Deloria seems to go even further than Basso in appealing to the potency of the places themselves over and above the occurrence of any important cultural events that might have taken place. This potency becomes particularly clear in his four-fold classification of sacred places.

Deloria describes four different types of sacred places in American Indian religion. Together these enable Indians to "look out along the four dimensions and locate their lands, to relate all historical events within the confines of this particular land, and to accept responsibility for it" (73). The first kind of sacred place illustrates that some places gain their sacredness by commemorating important events in tribal history or by being the site of ancestral burials. In these places, the land becomes sacred not just because of whatever might have happened to tribal members there but also because of the actual presence of the bones of the ancestors. To illustrate this first kind of sacred place, Deloria quotes a Crow Indian chief refusing to sell any more of his land to the federal government in 1912. The Crow chief told government negotiators, "[T]he soil you see is not ordinary soil—it is the dust of the blood, the flesh, and the bones of our ancestors. We fought and bled and died to keep other Indians from taking it, and we fought and bled and died helping the Whites. You will have to dig down through the surface before you can find nature's earth, as the upper portion is Crow. The land as it is, is my blood and my dead; it is consecrated; and I do not want to give up any portion of it" (148).

Deloria characterizes the second kind of sacred place as "locations where we have perceived that something specifically other than ourselves is present" (273). This nonhuman presence might reveal itself in the form of the miraculous arrival of some buffalo to feed a starving people or an aggressive bear letting itself be easily killed so that a tribe might bring an offering to a potlatch. These are places in which something of spiritual significance has appeared and inserted itself into a secular situation. The fact that the event is usually a surprise or a blessing for the people involved indicates that the place has taken on a little more agency of its own.

The other two kinds of sacred places ascribe even less importance to events in cultural history and more to the characteristics of the places themselves. The third type of sacred place consists of places holy in themselves, without regard to any historical occurrence involving activities of the tribe. Different kinds of landforms are often examples of the third type of sacred place. Mount Shasta in Northern California, for example, is one such sacred place. Devil's Tower in Wyoming is another. The fourth type of sacred place is land in which the people should be prepared to experience future revelations. The possibility of the continuing revelation of the sacred in tribal life means that some places must be protected just for the potential that they offer. Both the third and fourth type are sacred in themselves independently of any value that humans might ascribe to them. They do not rely on cultural events or history for any of their significance. These places have a spiritual agency of their own.

In this account of sacred places it is clear that some of the elements of the sacred manifest themselves only after long periods of continued inhabitation. Deloria does not underplay the significance of continuous long-term residency. He points out that thousands of years of occupancy of their lands have taught tribal peoples about the sacred landscapes for which they are responsible. He adds that immigrant cultures would eventually gain the same kind of religious connection to places if they would only stay put long enough. It is also clear from his account that cultural narratives play a crucial role in capturing the power of the place and ensuring that knowledge of the sacred is passed down through the generations. But what is most interesting about Deloria's account is how he places a lot of the emphasis on *the agency of the land independently of human affairs.* Places do not become active in tribal religion only as a result of human activities. Mount Shasta is a sacred site for the Shasta people not because they have made it so. The snows, the forests, and the animals that are the manifestations of its power in tribal stories are present on Mount Shasta regardless of whether there are people there to describe them. The power of the sacred place will inevitably become incorporated over time into tribal activity, figuratively through ritual and story and literally through ingestion of the plants and the animals that live there. But even before this occurs, Deloria insists that the land itself "must somehow have an unsuspected spiritual energy or identity that shapes and directs human activities" (148). The land already possesses its own agency, and this agency goes on to shape cultural religious belief. Deloria is not speaking figuratively when he claims "the mountains, rivers, waterfalls, even the continents and the earth itself have intelligence, knowledge, and the ability to communicate ideas" (152). This makes the natural world, as an agent in itself, "integral to human activities and ambitions" (154).

Basso's discussion of the Western Apache approach to morality and Deloria's account of Native American religions both suggest that knowledge practices of different kinds owe something to the particularity of the places in which that knowledge is constructed. These accounts appear to share something with a long forgotten insight latent, perhaps, in Plato's *Timaeus* and his *Phaedrus*. They also appear to confirm something that lab studies theorists, ecological psychologists, and some cognitive scientists acknowledge, namely that the materiality of the setting in which knowledge practices occur contributes something to the knowledge claims that are made. The physical environment is not just a site in which mind operates; it is a characterful place that influences the products of the mind.

Whether Deloria and Basso can be regarded as describing the same insight as the lab studies theorists and the ecological psychologists is not exactly clear. It seems a little unlikely. In lab studies, the influence of the materiality of the lab does not require thousands of years of residence and the handing down of culturally incorporated narratives before it attains its significance. In lab studies, the material environment that contributes is a highly artificial arrangement of spaces and instrumentation set up in order to answer a very specific set of questions about the behavior of certain aspects of physical reality. This contrasts sharply with the expansive natural environments about which Deloria and Basso are speaking. However, there is clearly some overlap between the two views. Knowledge claims emerge out of a complex interaction between cultural activities, social values, individual idiosyncrasies, the presence of the sacred, and the material arrangements of the physical environment. Both approaches make use of what Aristotle called "the marvelous potency of place."[24]

Engaging with Different Environments

In the broadening search for evidence in support of the grounding of knowledge, we have so far ventured into some fairly rarified territory in postmodern epistemology, some rather technical areas in cognitive science, and most recently into anthropology and religious studies. Does this mean that the grounding of knowledge is a purely academic endeavor? Is there a way to appreciate these points without wading through books published by academic presses? If these remarks about the significance of place are going to count outside of academic discourse, then it is important to move the discussion a little closer to home. This is not too difficult to do because the marvelous potency of place becomes immediately apparent, I suggest, to those who watch carefully what happens when they enter dramatic and unfamiliar physical territory.

Entering new and dramatic territory can make us realize the potency of place because of the shock it offers to cognitive structures that have grown accustomed to something different.[25] Just as sociologists of scientific knowledge have suggested that someone from outside the group is often needed to point out the biases shared by all the group members, so might it be necessary to go outside of your place to recognize just how cognitively wedded to it you have become. Such experiences offer what I call a "dislocating experience."[26] This is an experience in which, like Socrates drawn out of the city by Phaedrus, a person is both literally and metaphorically out of place. These kinds of dislocating experiences are interesting for at least the following two reasons. First, they illustrate just how much we are perceptually and cognitively grounded by our physical environments. The second, more suggestive reason is that these experiences might actually have an epistemic significance that enables them to be put to good use. The shock that a dislocating experience causes to the particular combination of values, practices, and perceptual habits to which we had adjusted can prompt a helpful revision of our entrenched ways of seeing the world. I return to this controversial suggestion in chapter 6. Here I offer only a personal account of what such a dislocating experience feels like.[27]

Not long ago, I spent a summer volunteering for the U.S. National Park Service in Dry Bay at the mouth of southeast Alaska's Alsek River, a fifty-mile bush flight from the nearest road. Dry Bay is on the seaward side of the glacier-covered peaks of the Fairweather Range, a range John Muir once described in his own characteristic way as "ineffably chaste and spiritual."[28] Mount Fairweather itself, which Muir called "the noblest and most majestic in port and architecture of all the sky-dwelling company," rises straight out of the ocean to 15,300 feet in the southeast. The Fairweather Range dominates the glacial outwash plane on which the forty or so summertime human inhabitants of Dry Bay reside. I was there to check the permits of rafters finishing their float of the Alsek and Tatshenshini Rivers.

On first moving to Dry Bay, I was both culturally and perceptually out of place. Dry Bay is the home of many brown bears, moose, and wolves and only a few part-time human residents. It has a long and fascinating Tlingit history.[29] The summer fishcamps that dot the banks of the Alsek and the East Alsek Rivers are removed before the darkness of winter sets in. It is a place of unusually massive scale. Visitors need time to adjust their perceptual faculties in order not to make grand errors of judgment. The mountain I saw to the north, Mount St. Elias, was not twenty but eighty miles distant, and the frigid, silty river at my feet was not flowing gently past, as it appeared, but racing by at a nine-knot clip. It seemed quite impossible that Mount Fairweather to the southeast could rise directly from the ocean to the height that locals assured me it did. A hike to its base would have been no small task itself due to the smaller range in front of it that was rendered invisible against Fairweather's massive flanks. Some local advice and caution were essential companions for the newly arrived.

While I was still in the throes of such a dislocating experience, it quickly became clear how perceptual experience happens both in and through places. I learned that my eyes did not recognize distances in the same way in different places. I soon realized that I would be absolutely incapable of judging either elevation or distance for a while. The idea of advising arriving bush pilots on the height of the cloud base terrified me until I had been instructed in some reliable rules of thumb for making these determinations using surrounding mountains. These visual confusions reached deeper than just my quantifications of distance and elevation. They resulted in a changed relationship to my environment. Despite possessing the same body, I was quite unclear what constituted near or far. In Dry Bay, it would have been almost unthinkable that I might get beyond the horizon within a day under my own steam, while in my hometown I do this nearly every time I get on my bike. When the ranger took me out "ranging" with him for a few hours on the Park Service ATVs, it was nearly impossible for me to conceptualize from my cabin where and how far we would go in relation to the land that I could see. Only by actually moving around the landscape for a few days did I begin to get some sense of where I was. On my return to my hometown a couple of months later, the perceptual confusion returned. Things seemed unusually crowded. The forested hill half a mile from my home seemed to be practically on top of me, because I had grown used to the scale of Dry Bay. The familiar Douglas firs that peopled my neighborhood drowned me beneath their deep columns for the first time.

The other senses were similarly shocked. In Dry Bay, the yipping of coyotes was the sound of the end of the summer day, replacing the sound of my roommate taking his dog out for a late-night walk. In my hometown, a creak in the night was the reassuring sound of my home contracting as the temperature changed. In Dry Bay, the same creak was a brown bear nosing around my cabin. Bringing with me to Dry Bay an excessive, culturally inscribed fear of the brown bear, I first turned every sound at night into an alarming reminder that I was really rather a small and powerless kind of a creature. But the longer I lived there, the more I became able to set that fear into the context appropriate for the place. My emotions as well as my senses needed time to settle into the new environment. As my perceptual skills adjusted over time to the landscape, my senses directed themselves toward different things. Sounds of the same volume were tuned in or out depending on their relevance to daily life in that environment. In Dry Bay, the Alsek River was first deafening and then silent as I grew used to living beside water. At the same time, my ears grew acutely sensitive to the sound of incoming planes. I could always hear them before the rafters who had just spent ten days on the river. Moving back to my hometown, the refrigerator was at first thunderously noisy at night, and then it slowly returned to being almost silent.

Dislocating experiences suggest that in moving to a new place there is a time period in which you have to learn how to sense in that place. It is obviously not that you no longer have the capacity to hear or see in the new place, but you do have to quickly train yourself in different perceptual skills, such as learning which of the sounds and sights are important. [30] Moving to a town with a middle-of-the-night train whistle will often keep a new resident awake until his or her body learns that it does not need to hear the whistle every time. In any environment we focus only on a portion of the data available to us, and we need a period of time in each new place to learn what this portion is going to be. This learning process itself is shaped by the kinds of activities we do and the kinds of physical realities—be they wandering moose or idling buses—that our environment presents to us. Greta Gaard has helpfully called this process one of "perceptual orienteering." [31]

Such observations suggest that when we are gathering knowledge through our senses, the place is not just incidental to the kind of gathering that occurs. The place influences not just *what* we perceive but also *how* we perceive what is there. The physical realities of the place combine with the cultural ideas that we bring to it to influence perception in a number of complex ways. It is not just the sense data that change when we change place but also the selection of the data as well as the skill at determining it. Freshly turned earth went almost unnoticed in my hometown, home of many moles, whereas in Dry Bay it was initially read as an important warning of brown bear activity.

These observations about this particular dislocating experience have so far been mostly about perception. But the thin line between perceptual and cognitive experience means that these perceptual challenges also translated into a deeper set of challenges to how I structured my world. My location in nature did not just affect what I perceived; it also challenged a number of the important categories that governed how my world was structured. I have already mentioned how the categories of near and far were transformed. Inside and outside were similarly scrambled. At home in a small town, outside is a place where I would go to find friends and have conversations; in Dry Bay I would mostly go inside to do this. Outside was also a place for some caution in Dry Bay due to unpredictable things such as wildlife and eroding riverbanks. Outside was initially associated with a certain amount of fear, being a realm of the unpredictable and the unfamiliar. As a result, my own identity shifted slightly due to the physical environment in which I was living. The territory that counted as home shrank in Dry Bay as the number of unknowns beyond the familiarity of my cabin was initially quite high. Home started to enlarge again as I became more comfortable in the area.

The forces that motivated my daily economy, the provision of food, the need to stay dry, the necessity of completing my Park Service responsibilities, acted out upon my body in ways different from the comparable forces in my hometown. For example, the provision of food in my hometown is almost always something mediated through money, by going to the ATM and then to the grocery store. It rarely manifests itself as an activity that connects me to the ecology of my place in any way. In Dry Bay, the provision of food was always accomplished socially by exchange with a rafter or a fisherman. Delicious wild raspberries and strawberries growing locally would occasionally supplement the exchange. Drinking water was collected off the roof, garbage burned, and human waste buried. Throughout the summer, the ecology of the region played itself out on my body and made its way into my body, in locally specific ways. My being-in-the-world, both physical and conceptual, took on a local character.

It would be hard to catalogue a precise set of direct causal relationships between the physical geography of Dry Bay and these perceptual and cognitive changes. Too many other factors were also at play in the way I experienced my physical and cultural environment that summer. Nor am I clear what kind of causal explanation of dislocating experiences like this one would be sufficient. I certainly would not turn to the natural sciences and expect them to explain everything about why distances looked so different in Dry Bay. Nor would I expect a social scientist to be able to tell the whole story. I also wonder what would have happened had I remained there for a number of years instead of only for two months. Would I have adjusted back to "normal" after some time and become cognitively and perceptually identical to how I am in my hometown? Or would I really have started to experience the world through a different lens? And was there anything about that dislocating experience that was cognitively beneficial to me? Was this dislocating experience epistemically significant in the sense that it might have made possible the creation of certain cognitive structures that I could not have created elsewhere? Though these questions are deliberately beyond my ability to answer, it is clear that Dry Bay had some kind of impact on my perceptual and cognitive life. The place worked its way into my mind and made things reappear in novel configurations. Dry Bay also persuaded me that being in the world as a cognitive and perceptual agent is a much more complicated matter than forming some universal, foundational skills and categories and building on those. Extremely dislocating experiences such as the one described give a hint that the particularity of place comes to influence a good deal more than just what happens to fall into our field of vision when we arrive in a new area.

PLACE OR MIND?

Observations similar to the ones that I have made about my Dry Bay experiences are not rare. Yi-Fu Tuan described the effects of physical settings on perception in his 1974 work *Topophilia*. He suggested that the straight lines of a carpentered world lead to different skills of perception than the jumbled lines found in natural landscapes.[32] He also suggested that unusual environments such as the high Arctic, where there is often little differentiation between the sky and the ice sheets, demand particular perceptual adaptation. The Inuit hunter, according to Tuan, navigates more by acoustic, olfactory, and sensory cues than by scanning the horizon for non-existent visual signposts. The Kalahari bush person becomes acutely sensitized to the presence of minute leaves indicating that edible roots can be found nearby. And the Polynesian sailor is finely tuned into the motion of the waves and currents under the boat. In these cases, the perceptual skills that become embodied over time are skills relative to particular environments. Colin Turnbull's study of the Mbuti people of the equatorial forest revealed how the perceptual skills of forest people do not function effectively in open grasslands. When brought out of the forest and onto an overlook, a Mbuti tribesperson who looked upon a herd of buffalo grazing several miles away saw the animals as insects. There was much knee slapping and belly laughing when Turnbull tried to convince the Mbuti man that these "insects" were the size of oxen.

Clearly perceptual skills are connected in certain ways to environments. But is this quite the significance of place for which we are looking? Are the environments really doing the interesting work here? Perhaps they are not. Most of the foregoing claims about peoples perceptually adjusted to their landscapes can probably be accommodated by an existing theory in contemporary epistemology known as the theory-dependence of observation thesis. If the perceptual adjustment can be explained this way, then it might not be necessary to make the strong claim that the place itself is directly influencing cognitive and perceptual structure.

The theory-dependence of observation thesis was first articulated by Norwood Russel Hanson back in 1958. Put in its most elegant form, the theory holds that "there is more to seeing than meets the eyeball."[33] Hanson argued that what we choose to observe in any situation is selected relative to a background set of theories and assumptions. Sense data are not just accumulated at random but are selected and sifted by what our theories have told us to expect. It *has to be,* or else we could never hope to make sense of such a complex jumble of information (a point related to one that Kant had appreciated two centuries previously). So we always operate with theoretical assumptions that prepare us to see certain things. Because our theories make us expect to see birds, we see a flock of starlings moving across the sky and not a single organism consisting of a hundred beaks and wing beats. We see certain things because those things fit better with what our theories have told us to expect. Hanson suggested that observation always is already theory-dependent.

A geographically informed version of the theory-dependence of observation thesis might be used to explain the phenomenon of being perceptually tuned into (or out of) certain landscapes. In this geographical version of the thesis, what we observe depends upon theories that we possess about the region in which we are making the observations. There are no brown bears in my hometown so I can drop the idea of being cautious when I run into freshly turned earth. I know that my hometown has no 15,000-foot mountains, so I don't need to learn the tricks that would allow me to correctly gauge their height. The Mbuti tribesperson does not need to be good at recognizing 1,500-pound ungulates in the jungle because there are none. These are the theoretical backgrounds that explain why we sense what we do. The objection to the strong claims I have made about place would then go something like this: "What you have described is not the landscape directly affecting perception and cognition but the human mind first cognitively grasping a theory about what to expect in an environment and then applying that theory to observation. Place is not affecting mind here. This is a mind that grasps certain things and then influences how the senses operate in light of that grasp. It is the theoretical grasp of the realities of the place that have caused the senses to behave in a certain way and not some direct influence of the place itself." So the Inuit hunter knows from experience that he will get lost if he relies on visual cues alone. The Kalahari bush person knows that scarce food has to sometimes be dug up from under the ground. These are good, cognitively appreciated reasons for people to keep their eyes open for some things and not for others. Over time, the senses adjust without the individual having to consciously recall the reasons why they should adjust. At this point, observations mistakenly appear to be shaped not by the theories brought to perception but directly by the geographies that ground them. But despite this appearance, the physical environment remains passive, and the human retains all the perceptual and epistemic agency. Any agency that one might be tempted to ascribe to the environments turns out to be really only a derivative of the agency of the discerning human presented through the theories that he or she has learned. If this objection stands, then places are not active in perception, and the human observer stays in control of what he or she sees.

A first response might be to question whether it is really a good objection at all. To say that a person has to hold a theory about the presence or absence of brown bears in an area before becoming cautious around freshly turned earth does not deny that features of the physical environment strongly influence how the person perceives his or her environment. It just questions how direct that influence is. The fact that the influence is filtered through a belief about the presence of bears does not mean the environment is not still playing a role in shaping perceptual skills. Since it is clear that culturally shared beliefs such as theories about the presence of food are also a part of the broader environment that shapes a knowledge claim, it is hard to think that the objection has real force. Only if you were concerned about maintaining a rigorous separation between physical causes coming directly from nature and causes coming from shared, culturally held beliefs about that part of nature would this objection have its intended power.

A second response might be to grant the legitimacy of the objection but to deny that it is comprehensive enough. Although the objection seems to work against some of the examples—the bears and the turned earth, the Inuit hunter and the nonvisual sensory cues—it does not appear to work as well for others. I might have needed a theory about the unpredictability of brown bears before I could be worried about freshly turned earth, but I did not need a theory for some of the other perceptual oddities of the dislocating experience. It *really did feel crowded* when I returned home from the glacial outwash plane to the trees in my hometown. The measurement of distance and space *really was harder* when I moved into Dry Bay. I did not have to possess any theoretical grasp of these places to feel this. These were embodied perceptual skills that did not rely on the theoretical grasp of any local knowledge. The embodied nature of the skills obviates the need for there to be any theory at work before place can affect perception.

Evidence exists to suggest that not only learned perceptual skills but also physiology itself sometimes adjust so as to tune perception into particular landscapes. Though it is taken to be obvious that people adjust physiologically to different environments by, for example, sweating more, getting a tan, or adding a layer of fat, it is rarely suggested that people also adjust perceptually to different environments. Yet the adjustments in physiology that this perceptual adjustment would require would be miniscule in comparison to the adjustments in physiology that are readily admitted. There is also some evidence that evolutionary processes can select for advantageous differences in perceptual ability. A study of young Inuit cited by Miles and Wallman found a predisposition to myopia that would not manifest itself as long as the children were exposed to the full range of the visual stimuli of their traditional childhood environment. [34] However, if these children spent the majority of their time in physical environments to which they were not culturally adjusted, then the myopia became a problem. It was found that in the time that books and audiovisual media had become the primary mode of education for Inuit children, the rate of myopia had increased to 50 percent of the general population. This appears to be an example of how not just observation but observers themselves are affected by the landscapes in which they reside. The perceptual skills had become embodied in people as a direct result of the environments in which they live and move.

The idea that a perceptual adjustment to environment can be physically embodied (either at an intra- or intergenerational level) takes us into some controversial territory. There is a good reason why claims about cognitive adjustment to particular environments are not often made. Connecting any aspect of perceptual or cognitive ability to the physical environment through causal laws has a sordid association with the environmental determinism proffered in the early twentieth century by overt racists such as Ellsworth Huntingdon. Environmental determinism has rightly been criticized for how it can be unscrupulously employed to make deterministic claims about the cognitive ability of people from different regions. The worst kinds of racism and sexism are often generated by deterministic claims of this nature.

Although environmental determinism is clearly something to worry about with claims like these, making physical location completely irrelevant also appears to me to be both undesirable and inconsistent. There are three remarks that I want to make about this. First, it is pure anthropocentrism, not to mention a remarkable act of faith, to suggest that humans and humans alone are able to completely transcend their physical environments in every perceptual and cognitive respect. Every other species is assumed without pause to have picked up certain of its physical characteristics from its environment. Dialectical biology in particular insists upon this. Not only does such a view draw an arbitrary line between human and nonhuman animals, but it also draws an artificial line between human perceptual and cognitive traits and human physical and muscular traits. Neither line is supportable in light of evolutionary theory. It also seems odd in an age in which entire books and journals are being devoted to discussion of a sense of place to deny the possibility of there being any trace of embodied, rather than rationally contrived, connection to the landscapes in which we choose to ground ourselves. Why deny that the grounding manages to get even skin deep? The trick—and this is a trick that a new genre of nature writers has absolutely mastered—is to look at the possibility of being connected to an environment as something positive rather than as something limiting. This should not be too difficult when one realizes that it is only centuries of philosophical prejudice in the Western tradition that have interpreted connections between mind and anything physical as a limiting factor rather than as a possibility for insight and innovation. Ties to place can be regarded as something to seek out rather than as something to avoid at all costs. Local vernacular and native character can be things to cherish, not to reject. Literature of many different kinds relies on this fact. The question of how to understand perceptual and cognitive connections to place as something positive and useful is the main topic of chapters 5 and 6.

Second, notice that it is very rare for environments to actually be different enough to make any significant difference to perception. I had to go from a semi-urban environment to Alaska to find a dramatic enough change in landscape to feel even slightly perceptually dislocated. It is more common not to notice any kind of perceptual adjustment between places. Places may count perceptually and cognitively, but it is rare that this is a very dramatic kind of effect.

Third, and perhaps most important for quelling fears of environmental determinism, notice the constant interplay of natural and cultural factors influencing perception. Natural factors never operate in isolation from cultural factors. Had I gone to Dry Bay with a different set of cultural biases, the influence of the place would have manifested itself in significantly different ways.

This means that for any determinative role that the place might try to play in perceptual or cognitive function, there are any number of layers of cultural factors that are also at work deflecting that determinism. When the implications of environmental determinism were first recognized, Vidal de La Blache quickly proposed a less harmful view he called "environmental possibilism." Environmental possibilism gives the environment some role, but not a determinative role, in shaping thought and belief. Possibilism suggests that environments offer possibilities and relative constraints but that humans are able to operate with a considerable degree of autonomy within those relative constraints. In Dry Bay, the place became influential toward, but in no way deterministic of, what went on in my mind. For one seeking to avoid the two extremes of environmental determinism on the one hand and complete detachment from physical influences on the other, the challenge is obviously to tell a story about the complexity of the relationship that individuals have with both their cultural and their physical environments. However this task is negotiated, it must be told as a story of opportunities and possibilities rather than one of limits and absolute constraints.

Compare the story told by Tuan to the one told earlier by Basso. Tuan comes across as the worst sort of environmental determinist when he connects the cosmology, the sense of time, and the social structure found in the Mbuti pygmies of the Congo rainforest and in Pueblo Indians of the American Southwest directly to the physical realities of their respective environments. Although Tuan certainly makes claims that resemble those of Basso, he posits a much more direct link between local environment, perception, and belief. Tuan makes local geography into an efficient cause of particular beliefs. One of his chapters outlines in simplistic form "the structuring of the world[view] based on the major physical characteristics of the habitat."[35] He actually specifies how the shape of the environment yields a particular type of belief. Basso paints a much more complex picture. He claims that environment is part of a relationship that also involves cultural practices, cultural histories, and sheer chance. Basso grants that a culture might have developed a completely different set of moral and religious strictures by creating different stories about their native lands. Tuan's claims do not so readily allow this. Tuan presents the place as offering direct causes, Basso presents it as offering possibilities. But Basso's account still incorporates the view that although belief structures are not completely determined by landscapes, nor are they totally unconnected to them.

A cultural geographer more careful than Tuan in appreciating the complexity of the relationship between environments and belief is David Sack. In

Homo Geographicus, Sack considered how notions such as place, world, and home operate in human lives. He claims that places work in a complex fashion to "draw together the natural, the social, and the intellectual" (12) in a way that is important for generating an understanding of how we are to function in the world. Like Tuan, Sack describes a place as something that has to be known by a culture through experience. In the process of being experienced, natural environments become places and start exerting their influence. Places "possess rules about the things to be included and excluded . . . they have meaning" (32). These cultural features of places combine with their physical features to exert an influence over social, natural, and intellectual forms. It is, says Sack, "the very fact that place combines the unconstructed physical space *in conjunction with* social rules and meaning . . . [that] enables place to draw together the three realms, and makes place constitutive of ourselves as agents" (33; emphasis added).

Sack's notion of place describes the relation between social values, cultural practices, and natural environments in a way that is complex enough to avoid the simple causal efficacy that Tuan ascribed directly to local geography. Sack's account also seems more descriptively accurate. The place I experienced in Dry Bay influenced me because it was a culturally and physically constructed environment rather than an entirely pregiven physical reality with a certain ecology. How it affected me depended both on facts about the physical environment and facts about my cultural assumptions. I had no idea what it was like to live among brown bears, but I brought numerous preconceptions with me. The places that Sack describes as being efficacious already include social rules and already involve human actions and intentions. From Sack's characterization of how place functions in our lives it should be clear that what the epistemologist needs is a sufficiently enriched and complex notion of place. Such an enriched notion is more suitable for making the connections between place and mind. But however complex the relation between geography, culture, and history might be, we should be careful to avoid letting the physical factors slip entirely from our view and disappear behind the cultural ones. In an anthropocentric culture such as our own, we need to be sure to hang on tightly to the marvelous potency of place.

To my way of thinking, these roadless areas, these
cores of remaining unprotected wildness, are the
best asset Montanans and Americans have going
for us. They filter the water, filter the air, and, if
you believe in such things, as I do—that a people's
culture is sculpted by its landscape—these
roadless areas filter and shape our spirits, too.
Any continuing harm we do to them harms
ourselves. And then we wonder where all our
anger and confusion comes from.

Rick Bass, "Getting It Right"

5 MAKING PLACE MATTER

The grounding of knowledge described in the last two
chapters suggests, at the very least, that it is important to recognize that physical environments are one of several parties operating in the complex set of
interactions out of which knowledge and ways of thinking get constructed. If
this is correct, then places have an important cognitive role to play. Statements
about sense of place should be regarded as not just romantic yearnings but as
statements that accurately reflect the fact that people craft some of their very
cognitive identity in communion with a landscape. Loss of the character of a
place should appear considerably more serious to people than is now generally
appreciated. Relocating to a different area should be recognized as a painful
time of mental reorganization rather than as a harmless change of scenery. We
should wonder less at the anger and confusion that Rick Bass claimed belong
to cultures that destroy the places in which they live.

Left relatively open so far has been the question of the precise causal role of
physical environments in these interactions. The question has been left open
largely because I am not entirely sure whether it is either desirable or possible
to be much more specific. It is clearly important to avoid the kind of envi-

ronmental determinism that would follow if epistemologists started to make claims of the form "environments of type X give rise to knowledge claims of type Y." It would also be an enormous task to try to adequately tease out the complex ways in which cultural histories and physical realities interact with each other in the production of knowledge. So many factors are simultaneously at work influencing what we say about the world that the desire to describe specific causal relationships between environment and belief should probably be resisted. That said, this book would lose some of its point were it not important to hold on tenaciously to the central claim that natural environments make significant contributions to the production of knowledge, contributions that it is important to understand if we are committed to richly situating knowledge. There may be ways of expressing these contributions that do them justice without overstating them. Philosopher of biology Christoph Rhemann-Sutter, for example, has argued that we can look at certain environments as combining with particular inherited traditions of ideas to become "more permissive" of some theories in biology than of others thanks to the way these environments are physically organized. [1] Like the environmental possibilism of de La Blache, this weakens the claim about the causal role of physical geography without completely eliminating it.

If the claim turns out to be this relatively weak one, then the question now arises about the kinds of uses to which such a claim can be put. Even if Shepard was right to suggest that there is an important connection between place and mind, if the connection is too weak and too vague, then it becomes doubtful whether the claim can be of any practical use. It might be philosophically satisfying to talk in general terms about a distinctive contribution of the physical environment to knowledge production, but it would remain unclear what this has really added to epistemology, to environmental philosophy, or to environmental policy and activism. Yet it seems that the recognition of the contribution of physical environments to knowledge does add something to each of these and, moreover, that it is something important. The remainder of the book is devoted to showing that these connections do, in fact, have significant normative implications for epistemology, environmental philosophy, and environmental policy.

A Strategic Intervention into Epistemology

The connections between place and mind described so far plug an important gap in contemporary discussions of naturalized and situated knowledge.

In plugging this gap, it can be argued that these connections add something of significance to contemporary epistemology. In order to show the positive value to epistemology of the connection between place and mind, it is necessary to go back to a remark made toward the end of chapter 4 and make good on the claim that being cognitively tied into particular places can turn out to be a positive thing rather than, as it might initially appear, something harmful and limiting. The argument requires revisiting some of the sociologies of science discussed earlier.

As was made clear in chapter 2, the vast majority of existing work on situating knowledge has been of a purely sociological variety. Sociologies of science have shown that science emerges from social and cultural situations that can often subtly—or not so subtly—infuse their biases into the work being done. So, for example, authors have shown how Victorian values infused much of nineteenth-century craniology, National Socialist values shaped Nazi studies of eugenics, and patriarchal values influenced certain accounts of evolutionary biology. The strongest claims emanating from the sociology of science suggest that all of science, and not just the science fanatically performed by scientists sponsored by particular ideologies, incorporates values in one form or another that influence its results.

Though some convincing detective work has certainly been done in discovering how scientific research has consistently fallen prey to the infusion of cultural biases, it has also been difficult to know exactly where to take this claim next. Are we stuck with the fact that every claim ever made in science will have a value bias? Are all of these values pernicious? Do different sciences and different societies vary in the degree to which they are open to the influence of value biases? Are there not some values that are more distorting than others? And if some values are inevitable in science and value neutrality is not a realistic goal, then what is the positive contribution of these sociological studies of science in the first place?

These questions concerning, on the one hand, the extent to which cultural values infuse science and, on the other, the nature of the impact of these values when they are present have been the source of a voluminous literature in the sociology of science. It is fair to say that hardly any of the questions in this interesting debate have been adequately resolved. Nor is it my intention to try to resolve them here. Fortunately, for current purposes, we need only to convince ourselves of the truth of one small fact in this debate in order to move the argument forward. We need only agree that *there exist at least some cases* in which cultural biases have without any doubt influenced the scientific endeavor and that they have done so in a harmful way. These would be the cases in which the alleged objectivity of science was replaced by an ideologically motivated inquiry that yielded dramatically distorted and harmful results. The work that has been done in the sociology of science to date puts this claim beyond any reasonable doubt. Even those scientists most committed to the possibility of value-neutral science will admit that there have been several cases of science that, in retrospect, have clearly been distorted by political ideology. Stephen J. Gould's *Mismeasure of Man* and Robert Proctor's *Racial Hygiene: Medicine under the Nazis* are both useful sources describing breathtakingly sexist and racist science that caused immeasurable harm.[2]

This single admission of the existence of some cases of distorted and harmful science is epistemically potent. Once we have accepted this minimal claim, then we are compelled to be on the alert against possible future cases in which values might also influence knowledge claims in similarly harmful ways. Being on the alert, it was suggested in chapter 2, requires always scrutinizing both the knowledge claim itself *and* the scientist making the knowledge claim for clues about how research might have taken one ideologically informed direction when it could have taken another. Feminist epistemologist Lorraine Code called it "taking subjectivity into account." Some skeptics will no doubt still question the need to take subjectivity into account on the grounds that scientific laboratories are already carefully designed to screen values out of the scientific process. But even these boosters of the purity of science will likely acknowledge the value of this precaution for knowledge claims that are made outside of the scientific laboratory. In the world of everyday experience and belief there are no mechanisms in place specifically to filter out subjective biases. Knowledge claims made outside the lab are much more likely to include our prejudices. In fact, taking subjectivity into account outside of the scientific laboratory is probably something that most people are accustomed to doing every day as a basic rule of thumb in social interaction.

Feminist epistemology has distinguished itself by the effort and care that it has taken to reveal the hidden subjectivities that might potentially plague knowledge claims. First and foremost among hidden subjectivities for feminist epistemologists, not surprisingly, has been gender. But feminists have long recognized that gender is not a monolithic construction that affects all those in a given location in the same way. Gender operates as just one of a diverse collection of social locations, each of which exerts its own force on a person's experience. In addition to gender, feminist analysis has revealed that race, ethnicity, class, religion, and sexuality must also be taken into account for their potential to add a hidden subjectivity to a knowledge claim. These subjectivities are neither always bad nor always eradicable. It is just that ignorance of how they might be operating can lead to claims not being appropriately contextualized or situated.

The number of hidden subjectivities that need to be taken into account is not fixed ahead of time. Some feminist scholarship has taken the form of systematically uncovering the range of different subjectivities that are relevant. If the goal of these inquiries is to make visible all of the potential distortions in knowledge claims, then it is presumably important to uncover as many different sources of distortion as possible. There seems no reason to assume that race, ethnicity, class, religion, and sexuality are the only epistemic locations that can introduce values into a knowledge claim. Political persuasion, age, and level of physical mobility might also be significant epistemic locations particularly as you get further and further from the laboratory. Being open to the possibility that there are other as yet undiscovered hidden subjectivities seems like a prudent attitude in postmodern epistemology.[3]

Herein lies the shortcoming of existing work. Up to this point, the hidden subjectivities that feminist epistemologists have been prepared to consider have included only locations in a given *social* structure, a structure that has typically been characterized by these epistemologists as patriarchal, capitalist, racist, and heterosexist. It has not unreasonably been assumed that if a value is being imported into a knowledge claim, it is bound to be a value that is a product of a person's place in the existing social order. Values are shared by social groups so it has seemed plausible that they have their genesis entirely within those groups, but such an assumption confuses the source of the value with the vehicle through which the value operates. Even if it is a social group that holds or carries a value, the social group does not necessarily bear all the responsibility for having created that value. The source of the value might lie elsewhere. Completely ignoring other potential sources of value is an error.

There are a number of good reasons why feminist epistemologists and theorists representing other marginalized groups should have focused their analysis exclusively on the influence of various social orderings on values. One obvious reason is that the social order is the thing in need of being reformed. Feminist analysis typically attempts to contribute to the goal of reforming oppressive social structures so that they are less sexist, less racist, and less heterosexist. For this reason the whole critique from beginning to end has tended to remain focused exclusively on those social structures. A second good reason why feminists have focused on the social sources of values is that social orders actually have the potential to be deconstructed and reconstructed along better lines when the political will allows it. It would appear that, if a part of the natural order were contributing a value bias, there would be little point in trying to critique it. The relative fixity of the natural order is something that cannot so easily be reconstructed. In fact, apparently fixed natural orders have for that very reason traditionally been used by sexists, racists, and heterosexists to legitimate some of the very oppression to which postmodern and feminist theorists are objecting. Feminists have spent years helpfully problematizing the association of femininity with biology. They are rightly reluctant to consider that another natural ordering such as the physical environment might operate as an epistemic location.

Despite these very good reasons for keeping the focus on the social order, there is also a major problem with an analysis that simply refuses to consider any aspect of the natural order as a relevant part of an individual's epistemic location. The problem lies in the anthropocentric refusal to be accountable to our ecological situation. In current approaches, social considerations have utterly eclipsed ecological and evolutionary ones. Sophisticated, postmodern analysis has ended up being almost totally blind to something absolutely elemental about our existence. Epistemologists who stick to social biases risk concerning themselves so much with intrahuman discourse that they completely lose sight of the earth. Such a discourse dissociates itself dangerously from the physical world that it seeks to describe. Language assumes all the burden of creating the reality of our ecological situation. The endless play of words that results is both frustrating and exhausting. It leaves us with a feeling that Albert Borgmann has described as the "listlessness" of the postmodern condition.[4] This listlessness is the product of a pessimism about ever being able to concretely connect with material reality. Environmental philosopher Jim Cheney has accurately characterized the situation as one that creates a disengaged and politically impotent subject "freely creating world upon world of words—finally not taking any responsibility for its words but merely pouring them forth in conversation after conversation."[5] From an environmentalist's perspective, granting this epistemic distance between the worlds we create with our words and the worlds we actually inhabit with our bodies is extremely worrying. The same arrogance that claimed for humans the possibility of a view from nowhere in modern epistemology reappears here in perhaps even more virulent form. Humans can now do better than simply knowing the world objectively with absolute detachment; they can literally speak it into existence through sophisticated word games. Accountability fades, creating a recipe for ecological disaster. The insistence that the relevant parts of our epistemic locations are exclusively social is the source of this disaster.

The corrective that is needed for this anthropocentric flaw in contemporary epistemology is to bring these discussions back down to earth by reintroducing the natural. This neglect of the natural up to this point should be a theoretical red flag because it reflects a residual human-centeredness in postmodern accounts of knowledge. This anthropocentrism should be of concern to both the environmentally minded and the non-environmentally minded postmodern epistemologist because anthropocentrism remains one of the defining characteristics of the view that postmodernists are attempting to supercede. The corrective would begin to remedy what Andy Pickering has called the neglect of the material in studies of knowledge.

Reintroducing the natural into this discourse is no doubt a threatening prospect for those who have wisely learned to fear the suggestion that environment or biology in any way influence how we see the world. Environmental and biological determinism, as already mentioned, both have racist and sexist histories. But once again the trick is to achieve the reintroduction of the environmental part while avoiding the determinism part. This is no doubt a delicate negotiation, but it is an important and necessary one. Even some feminist epistemologists, a group as cognizant as any of the dangers involved, have begun to lament their peers' insistence on the exclusion of every natural factor from their discourse. Carol Bigwood has looked at the way Judith Butler socially constructs both sex and gender in *Bodies That Matter* and remarked "what is most disturbing and dangerous . . . is [Butler's] complete abandonment of nature and support of purely cultural determinants in the construction of gender. . . . [Nature] has lost any independent non-anthropocentric status to become merely the product of human action . . . reduced to a cultural idea."[6] Bonnie Mann has worried about how the "emphatic anti-essentialism" of recent feminist theory has led to an unhelpful alienation from the very world that sustains us from moment to moment.[7] Nancy Tuana has described in some detail how the material locations that she occupies should be regarded as every bit as much a part of the place from which she speaks as her social locations.[8] Each of these feminist authors has recognized that the diligence with which other feminist theorists have sought to avoid connecting epistemic identity to anything remotely physical has come with a cost attached to it. Part of this cost is to blind us to the fact that we are woven into the ecology of a planet that is the source and ground for absolutely everything that we do. We need as many ways as possible of learning that we do not float entirely free of this ground. Another part of the cost is that the emphatic rejection of the physical has become an obstacle to any interesting discussion of how to carve out crucial discursive and political spaces amid the physical realities of bodies that Annette Baier called "marvelously corporeal" and of environments that Ed Hutchins called "rich in organizing resources."

Reintroducing natural determinants does not have to be as regressive as it appears. This is because the discussions of natural factors that will be appropriate are only those that consider factors such as body and place to be neither wholly natural nor wholly deterministic. Consider again what David Sack said about places in chapter 4. Places draw together the natural, the social, and the intellectual in such a way that they give us a location from which to understand the full complexity of our relationships to what lies around us. Places already contain social rules and meaning when they come to exert their influence on us. This means that although places count as natural determinants due to the physical forces they contain, it is not possible to understand their influence independently of the cultural determinants that are also already at work. There is no place entirely free from culture, and so there is no natural determinant that is exclusively natural. This makes the problematic kind of naturalism that excludes any kind of cultural influence unlikely.

Not only are places not fully natural, but neither are they fully deterministic. If places were fully deterministic, then their influence would operate mechanistically on us according to the physical laws of nature. Just as genes and environment are not fully deterministic in dialectical biology, neither are places fully deterministic in naturalized epistemology. As we saw in Basso's discussion of the Western Apache, once the cultural indicators have been laid atop the physical ones, there is a certain amount of flexibility and chance involved in just how places influence us. It is possible that the same place might have a number of different influences on a particular people depending on just how the distribution of meaning in the place had occurred. Some places will be more permissive of particular kinds of influence on us than others without anyone ever actually being able to fully determine the nature and strength of the influence. Possibilism is importantly different from determinism.

The need to turn away from modernist and anthropocentric fantasies of detachment is a major reason why it is important for epistemologists to consider physical location as one of the possible hidden subjectivities in a knowledge claim. Pretensions of detachment mask desires to control, and in this case the desire leaves us suffering from the dangerous illusion that we float free of the ecological realities of the planet that sustains absolutely everything we do. But it is possible to say more than simply that the reintroduction of natural factors relieves us of these harmful illusions and that the reintroduction can be done in a nonproblematic way. We can add that recognizing the earthly grounding of knowledge actually turns out to be positive in certain important ways. It is not just a good thing to know about an epistemic location when it exists. It is possible to turn physical location into something socially and epistemically advantageous. There is at least one feminist epistemologist who has begun the discussion of why this should be the case.

In her recent book *Is Science Multicultural?* Sandra Harding recognized that once you have taken science studies insights outside of the lab, natural environments begin to look like they might make positive contributions to the manufacture of knowledge. Harding has long been one of the most vocal advocates of identifying the hidden subjectivities that give every knowledge claim a particular location. She characterizes those hidden subjectivities as falling under "categories of localness." She has picked out four broad supercategories of localness that influence scientific practice: "culturally distinctive interests," "ways of organizing knowledge production," "discursive traditions," and "location in heterogeneous nature."[9] The importance of these supercategories across different cultures leads her to suggest that all of science should be regarded as indigenous knowledge—indigenous because it is always constructed locally, relative to these four supercategories. The last of these four is obviously of the most interest in the current argument.

Harding notes how a culture's location in heterogeneous nature exposes it to a unique set of natural forces. "Some cultures daily interact with high altitudes and others not; some with mountainous terrains, deserts, oceanic islands, rain forests, or rivers; some interact with extremely cold and others with extremely hot climates; some with one range of diseases and health hazards, and others with quite a different range" (62). She adds that biological differences (which she hurriedly footnotes as often being socially constructed) such as skin pigmentation and relative immunity to malaria also make possible different interactions with surrounding environments. In no account of the physical particularities that affect us should these natural factors be treated as static. Cultures move, climates change, and cultural practices evolve. But in acknowledging location in heterogeneous nature as an important site of analysis, Harding makes a start on recognizing the significance of place to thought and belief. She wisely leaves it pretty vague just how places come to play the role that they do. She speculates that "cultures living on the edges of continental plates might well find the geology of plate tectonics more plausible (and 'interesting'!) than do cultures with little experience of earthquakes, volcanoes and other phenomena characteristic of plate-juncture environments" (64). But despite the vagueness and the qualifying footnotes, Harding's account is notable for how the physical environment gains a place alongside cultural interests and practices in her discussions of how knowledge is situated.

The insightful, normative move that Harding makes next is to configure this connection to heterogeneous nature so that it can be viewed as something positive rather than as something limiting. She insists that local specificity "could, should, and does have positive effects on the growth of knowledge" (62). The kind of locatedness that heterogeneous nature provides turns out to be an important tool for the possibility of better knowledge. This means treating cultures, in their location in nature, as what she calls "toolboxes" rather than "prison houses" for scientific knowledge. Locations can provide valuable sources of insight rather than placing limits on the knowledge that can be produced. Those living and working on boats have a relation to the ground and to stability that is simply not available to those living and working on land. Different forms of insight are available to those living in sparsely populated deserts as opposed to dense northern urban areas. Hidden subjectivities that are place specific provide possibilities denied to those who would claim to know from nowhere. A limited view limits distractions and makes possible organic solutions to problems that come out of a place rather than one-size-fits-all solutions imposed from without. In Harding's hands, the connection between place and mind turns out to be a positive force. She argues that a partial perspective in postmodern epistemologies can sometimes be a privileged perspective rather than something to be embarrassed about.[10]

We can also note of Harding's position that it illustrates how indigenous cultures in their native environments are particularly rich sources of insight into certain problems. Immigrant cultures rarely have the benefit of the extended inhabitation of one place necessary for the influence of that place to infuse into the full range of the culture's beliefs and practices. It will likely do little good to look at persons recently transplanted to Santa Fe from Seattle to determine how the character of the new natural environment affects their knowledge claims. Though they would probably be struggling through an interesting dislocating experience, they will be unlikely to have yet developed any geographically distinctive knowledge practices. It does, however, make sense to ask the same questions of a Western Apache woman in Cibecue who has inherited knowledge practices handed down through many centuries of residence on the same land. What increases the importance of this extended inhabitation even more is its increasing rarity. There are a rapidly diminishing number of intact indigenous cultures left resident on their native land. This makes their continued loss and the continued lack of interest in creating economically viable ways for indigenous peoples to stay on their native land painful for epistemic reasons among all the many others.

The positive spin that Harding puts on location in nature as a category of localness illustrates how epistemologists can join nature writers in their belief that being connected to a physical environment can be something to cherish rather than a sign of limitation and parochialism.[11] Grounding knowledge is not only a valuable counter to anthropocentrism in epistemology; it is also a guard against postmodern listlessness. Being tied into a place is not a source of backwardness that romantics mistakenly bless with nostalgia; rather, it is a sign of being fully integrated into a way of being in the world. Taking place seriously in epistemology is one important way to affirm the significance of people for *what* they are *where* they are.

A Strategic Intervention into Environmental Philosophy

If the connection between place and mind looks like it can serve a helpful and important purpose in contemporary epistemology, can it do the same in environmental philosophy? Studies in cognitive science, the philosophy of mind, and epistemology have generally seemed to be of only peripheral interest to the business of environmental philosophy. In its short history, environmental philosophy has concerned itself primarily with ethics. For better or for worse, many of the central debates in environmental ethics have revolved around the question of whether there are good arguments to be made for the existence of intrinsic value in nature, value that exists independently of the consciousness of any beings who might be found there. Early on, environmental philosophy was more or less defined as the quest to adequately articulate a non-instrumental ethical relationship toward nature in which the presence of natural value could serve as a constraint against the destruction of ecological diversity for human gain.

These discussions in ethics have seldom seemed to be in any way connected to discussions in epistemology or in the philosophy of mind.[12] When environmental philosophers have made these connections, it has usually been in the context of their discussions of the worldviews of indigenous peoples. But as pointed out in chapter 4, non-indigenous environmental philosophers have been criticized for the way they have used insights taken from indigenous philosophies. These criticisms suggest that it is important for non-indigenous environmental philosophers to try to find a different route into the connection between place and mind.

There are good reasons to make the search for this new route quite central to environmental philosophy. The current lack of any sustained discussion of epistemology or the philosophy of mind in environmental philosophy looks odd indeed when you consider that many of those debates in ethics with which environmental philosophy has been preoccupied have at their center some important assumptions about rationality and belief. Ethical anthropocentrism—often cast as environmental philosophy's nemesis—has deep roots in the Western philosophical canon. These roots are connected to a number of unquestioned and sorely underdiscussed assumptions about rationality and belief. Failure to challenge these assumptions leaves the antienvironmental anthropocentrist with too easy and traditional an avenue for response.

Anthropocentrism in mainstream ethics has close links to the view shared by both Plato and Aristotle that humans can be distinguished from the rest of nature primarily by their possession of the capacity to reason. Aristotle first considered nutrition, growth, and sensation as distinctively human activities but concluded that each of these capacities was shared with plants or animals. The distinctively human activity, Aristotle asserted, was "an activity of soul which follows or implies a rational principle." [13] Having found this distinguishing characteristic, Aristotle used it as the starting point for his ethics. The ultimate goal for a human seeking the good life was to perform its distinctive rational function well. Rationality was lodged at the very heart of Aristotelian ethics.

Though it is certainly not the case that every ethicist who followed Aristotle made rationality so central to his theory—Immanuel Kant did, David Hume did not—the idea that the most notable distinction between humans and the rest of nature was the former's ability to reason and the latter's inability remained deeply imbedded in the tradition. More often than not, this distinguishing feature was also assumed to have moral relevance. René Descartes distinguished humans from nonhuman nature by suggesting that humans were made up of both physical substance and thinking substance whereas nonhumans were made up of only physical substance. Things possessing only physical substance such as trees and animals could be treated like machines with no need for any particular moral regard. Descartes managed to persuade himself that, due to its lack of any thinking substance, the squealing of a dog during a vivisection experiment was a purely mechanical reaction involving no conscious feelings of pain or discomfort on the dog's part. Kant thought that the only moral reason to avoid treating an animal badly was that such behavior might by force of habit encourage humans to start treating other humans badly. The animal itself was owed nothing. Sometimes reason appeared in a moral theory under the guise of the ability to use language, the ability to imagine a future and contemplate the past, or the ability to understand God's will. Though subtly hidden in these cases, reason stayed relatively central to ethics.

Occasionally moral theorists managed to avoid using rationality or its surrogates as a criterion of moral worth by selecting something entirely different, such as the ability to feel pleasure or pain, as a replacement criterion. But even in these alternative theories, the relevance of rationality to morality was often retained in some form. Even if it was pain that was understood to be what counts morally, it was still typically assumed that a creature needed to possess rationality in order to effectively use that criterion. Rationality was necessary to reason impartially that another creature's pain was as undesirable as one's own and to calculate whether a proposed action would cause a balance of pain over pleasure. So even when not held up specifically as the ultimate determinant of moral considerability, rationality still usually retained considerable significance in the ethical arena. Greek assumptions about rationality have clearly had a massive influence on ethics.

Other theorists have shown how these same assumptions about rationality have influences on the environment reaching far beyond ethical theory. In *Feminism and the Mastery of Nature*, Val Plumwood identified a pattern of dualistic thinking that permeates some cultures and is implicated in their destructive attitudes toward nature. Dualistic thinking involves setting up two mutually exclusive categories that come to be treated as not only different from each other but also oppositional. Plumwood characterized dualistic thinking as "an alienated form of differentiation, in which power construes and constructs difference in terms of an inferior and alien realm" (42). Subsequent to the construction of the dualism, one side is typically given a higher value than the other. This hierarchy is then used to legitimate the subordination of the category valued lower by those in the category valued higher. Dualisms such as those between men and women, white and nonwhite, civilized and noncivilized, have led to social systems that are inherently oppressive to the devalued group. Plumwood blames dualistic thinking for creating "logics of colonization." Ecofeminist Karen Warren gives dualistic thinking a similarly central role in supporting "oppressive conceptual frameworks."[14] According to both these ecofeminist thinkers, Western masculinist thinking is permeated by a whole set of interrelated and mutually reinforcing dualisms that create a fault line through contemporary society. Dualisms between culture and nature, reason and emotion, male and female, universal and particular, human and animal, have become mutually enfolded and reinforcing of each other. But there is one dualism in particular that Plumwood suggests has been central to the creation of all the others. This is the dualism between reason and nature.

Plumwood argues that the reason/nature dualism is the pivotal dualism in what she calls "the rationalistic tradition." This tradition runs throughout the history of Western philosophy and champions rationalistic values of abstraction over particularity, necessity over contingency, and opposition over connection. Part of the origin of the rationalistic tradition is the familiar Greek view that reason is what distinguishes humans from animals. Plumwood makes it clear that the kind of challenge to the rationalistic tradition that she has in mind involves a fairly comprehensive revisioning of things. It requires more than just starting to give a bit more consideration to whatever lies on the devalued side of the dualisms. It would not be particularly helpful to simply elevate the importance of nature over and above that of reason because this would leave most of the structure of the dualism intact. The challenge involves looking again at both sides of the dualism in order to rethink the division itself. After all, the dualism rests on a series of questionable a priori assumptions made nearly two and a half thousand years ago on the basis of some rather sketchy evidence about the nature of mind.

One way to begin this revisioning would be to question whether the division is quite as abrupt as it was once thought. Darwinian evolutionary theory can provide a helpful springboard for doing just that. Evolutionary theory leads us to question whether there can be a radical discontinuity between capacities alleged to be possessed by humans but not by nonhumans. One of the important lessons to draw from evolutionary theory is that differences of degree are more common in nature than differences in kind. This makes it likely that rationality does not supply an entirely clear-cut dividing line between human and nonhuman nature. Cognitive ethology is a relatively new discipline devoted to the investigation of precisely this question of whether certain organisms in nonhuman nature can reason.[15]

But using Darwinian evolutionary biology to blur the boundary between the human and the nonhuman may not be enough to undermine the dualism at the heart of the rationalistic tradition. Knowing the story that Darwin told does not seem to alter the fact that humans manage to do some significant things that nonhumans do not. They send rockets to the moon, they study calculus, and they engage in discussions of moral theory. These are all things that nonhuman creatures appear to be incapable of doing. Even Darwinian differences of degree can still sometimes be important differences. Daniel Dennett, for once, declares that even though human minds evolved out of nonhuman precursors, there yet exists "a huge difference between our minds and the minds of other species, a gulf wide enough even to make a moral difference."[16] Perhaps the human capacity to reason has developed enough that it *is* significantly different from any capacities found in nonhuman nature. This suggests that something in addition to the Darwinian argument may be needed to undercut the dualism between the rational and the nonrational that props up the inherited tradition.

An alternative method of undercutting the dualism emerges out of the grounding of knowledge. Rather than suggesting that the fault line between the rational and the nonrational does not lie where originally thought, an alternative strategy is to look at the activity of reasoning itself and to show that it is an activity that by its very nature connects us to, rather than separates us from, the nonrational parts of nature. Rationality does not then represent a point of alienation from nonrational nature but one of integration with it. Overcoming the Cartesian view of rationality as some ghostly presence located deep inside, and functionally independent of, the body and the environment significantly changes how we look at the reason/nature divide. As empirical studies of mind have granted increasingly more significance to embodiment, and as epistemology has become increasingly more richly naturalized, reason has started to look like an activity of engagement and involvement with the world rather than of detachment from it. If the rational can no longer be isolated from the nonrational parts of nature by being entirely sealed off inside the human skulls, then the Greek assumptions that have worked to sustain the radical separation of the rational from the nonrational parts of nature start to crumble. The sequence of dualisms that Plumwood identified as resting on the Greek assumptions fall shortly thereafter. Nonrational nature can then start to be regarded as an integral part of mind rather than an oppositional foil for it. This has numerous implications not only for the assumptions that sustain the dualisms of the rationalistic tradition but also for the use of rationality in ethics in general.[17]

There is a way to draw some of these implications neatly into the existing lexicon of environmental ethics. It involves introducing the category of the cognitive or epistemic value of nature and adding this category to the list of other values nature supports. Environmental ethicist Holmes Rolston III has offered a useful typology characterizing each of the different values found in nature.[18] Some of these values are instrumental, some intrinsic, and some systemic. The position that he is most famous for articulating is that nature contains objective intrinsic and systemic values, values that exist independently of the uses to which they can be put by human and other conscious organisms.

It takes Rolston a certain amount of work to show what it is for a value to exist objectively in nature rather than simply in a person's mind.

Rolston typically begins his case for the existence of values in nature with subtle shifts in language in order to open up doors for later arguments. So, for example, when he surveys the different ways that people value nature, he describes these as values not given to nature by humans but values *carried by* nature. In Rolston's view, using this language enables him to "make an inventory of how nature is valuable to humans, with the subtle advantage that the term *carry* lets us switch-hit on the question of objectivity and subjectivity."[19] These might be values that exist only for us to take advantage of, or they might turn out to be values that actually exist independently of us. Some of the fourteen values that he describes (including economic, recreational, and aesthetic) are clearly valued relative to their uses for humans, whereas others (such as life and diversity) seem to be valued for what they are in themselves. A fifty-year-old plantation-grown Norwegian spruce tree can be valued for the lumber it supplies for building houses, whereas a thousand-year-old giant sequoia tree can be valued simply for what a magnificent creature it is.

Rolston moves toward intrinsic and systemic values by arguing that in all cases people find nature *valu-able* only because nature is something that is *able-to-carry-value*. Humans have the good fortune to be in the position to recognize these values where they exist, but such recognition occurs only in response to facts that are already present in nature. Even in cases when the values are most clearly instrumental, such as the nutritional value of the antelope to the lion or the spiritual value of the old-growth forest to the hiker, nature still cannot be valued merely as a resource. There must be something special about nature that makes it valu-able as a resource. Instrumental values can therefore never be entirely separated from intrinsic and systemic values. The former always rest upon the latter. Something is a resource only because it was already a source of value prior to the time at which another creature captured that value and made it into a resource.

Turning this language to the discussion of place and mind encourages us to look at places as supplying something that is a source of value for the functioning of mind. According to Mark Johnson's account of the embodied mind, cognition depends upon "structures that emerge from our experience as bodily organisms functioning in interaction with an environment."[20] Environments are thus instrumentally useful for the mind. They offer important structure that the mind borrows as it goes about its cognizing activity. This strongly suggests that we should value environments as cognitive or epistemic resources. But even to put it in this language of the environment offering "resources" for the mind overstates the instrumentality of place relative to mind. The dialectical relationship between place and mind articulated in chapter 3 means that mind does not pre-exist place and then utilize it as a resource in order to expand its already existing capabilities. The physical environment is not just an instrument for mind but a source of the very possibility of its existence in the first place. As Mark Rowlands argued in his account of psychotectonic externalism, the physical environment supplies some of the very architecture of mind and is integrated into some of its very processes. Mind thus depends on place rather than merely uses it. Places are part of the source of our rational capacities from the very beginning. This must also be part of their value. Hence environments should really be regarded as cognitive or epistemic *sources* rather than mere resources.

One of the fourteen values that Rolston thinks nature carries is "scientific value," because nature is "interesting enough to justify being known."[21] But the connection between place and mind suggests that nature is not just something that warrants being known; it is also the very ground and horizon of all knowing. Just as humans could not survive without the nutritional value that nature provides their bodies, so could they not think without the cognitive value that nature supplies their minds. Shepard was more or less right about this. Nature is not only of ecological value to us; it is also of psychological value.

Taking nature seriously for its role in making rationality possible allows us to add to Rolston's list of fourteen values another way that humans should value nature. In addition to valuing it for its recreational, economic, diversity, and life-supporting values, humans should also recognize nature for its cognitive or epistemic value. This is the value carried by nature that makes cognition and knowledge possible. As is the case with all valuable sources, these values should be identified and protected. Rolston already says of the impressive functioning of the human organism that "the skin-out processes are not just the support; they are the subtle source of the skin-in processes. In the complete picture, the outside is as vital as the inside."[22] The skin-in process of cognition finds its subtle source outside in the world. Moreover, it is beginning to seem less likely that cognition is entirely a skin-in affair after all, adding a certain level of complexity to the question of where cognitive or epistemic value falls in the typology of intrinsic, instrumental, or systemic values. Perhaps it is best to take a leaf out of Rolston's book and to switch-hit on this question for now.

Caveat

Though the last two chapters have been an attempt to shepherd the discussion toward natural environments, the way this has been done has included a certain amount of disingenuity. For, in fact, the arguments of the earlier part of the book suggest that all places, not just natural places, are of cognitive or epistemic value to us. Physical structures play organizing roles whether they are found in laboratories or in rainforests. Place and mind are connected as much in Manhattan as they are in an arctic village. We have not quite got an argument for preserving natural places yet, only an argument for preserving places in general. Some places, such as urban ghettos and nuclear power plants, we might not want to preserve. Others, such as saltwater marshes and tall grass prairies, we should be working hard to protect. This means that we need to add something to the argument in order to see why to preserve natural places in particular.

At this point Paul Shepard would no doubt want us to return to the claim that natural environments are the ones in which we evolved and therefore the ones that we can trust to provide the right kinds of organizing structures. There is a certain plausibility to his position, though it might leave us wondering whether those historic structures are the only ones that can ensure proper cognitive function. What if we simply do not have any of those structures left? And what of those people who voluntarily choose not to live among them? Although I grant Shepard's evolutionary arguments some credence, it would be better to construct an argument in favor of protecting natural places that does not so strongly impugn the value of nonnatural places. Chapter 6 is an attempt to supply an epistemological argument for supporting activist efforts to preserve nature with all its richness, integrity, and diversity, rather than to continue to replace it with homogeneous strip malls, suburban housing, and highways.

When we enter the landscape to learn something,
we are obligated, I think, to pay attention rather
than constantly to pose questions. To approach
the land as we would a person, by opening an
intelligent conversation. And to stay in one place,
to make of that one long observation a fully
dilated experience. We will always be rewarded
if we give the land credit for more than we
imagine, and if we imagine it as being more
complex even than language.

Barry Lopez, *The Rediscovery of North America*

6   PRESERVING PLACE AND MIND

Chapter 5 outlined some of the positive contributions that
the ideas articulated in this book make to the academic disciplines of epistemology and environmental philosophy, respectively. It included recommended modifications and additions to contemporary studies of knowledge
and to contemporary debates about the moral relationship of humans to nature. As is often the case in academic discourse, the practical consequences
of these recommendations for nonacademics might not be particularly obvious. Do specific policy recommendations follow from the abstract, academic
claim that place is a hidden subjectivity in knowledge or that the environment
should be valued as a cognitive or an epistemic source? Or is this just philosophy for its own sake, leaving environmental policymakers with no additional
tools or arguments to further their case?

In the face of this worry, the philosopher might first suggest in his or her
own defense that abstract philosophical conversations like these do eventually
permeate down through culture. New ideas first articulated in universities, if
they are good ones, eventually seep out of closeted academic spaces and gain
wider acceptance throughout society. The philosopher might point out that it

was thanks to people such as Plato and Descartes that we became cognitively disconnected from the earth in the first place, so it is the task of other philosophers to figure out how to set about fixing this mistake. It is the philosopher's obligation, so this response might go, to keep his or her discourse in the abstract in the hope that he or she can articulate clear principles that can trickle down and inspire others who are more talented at creating change outside of the academic realm.

This philosopher's hope for a trickle-down effect from his or her recommendations is fortunately not the only kind of practical guidance that the grounding of knowledge can supply. It is fortunate because environmental philosophy is already often under fire for its profusion of fancy words and its paucity of concrete contributions to policy. In addition, the talk of a trickle-down effect is elitist and offensive wherever it is found. If this were all that the philosopher had to conclude from this discussion, then he or she should rightly be criticized for it. But the philosopher does not need to rely on the hope of some vague trickle-down effects, because there is a specific policy implication that follows directly from the linkage between place and mind. This recommendation is consistent with arguments that can be made from a number of other environmental perspectives. As such it should be regarded as *additional* support for existing environmental policy rather than as a radical new proposal. The specific policy recommendation that follows from the grounding of knowledge is that communities should actively endeavor to maintain the full natural diversity—by which I mean the biodiversity, the cultural diversity, and the geographical diversity—of all the places in which their beliefs might get formed. The importance to epistemology of protecting a diversity of natural places rests upon the role that diversity plays in creating more critical knowledge.[1] There are several different kinds of arguments that one can make for the importance of diversity in epistemology. Brief outlines of three of these arguments follow.

Advocates for diversity in knowledge projects typically mean a range of different things when they talk about diversity. Sometimes they mean that it is important to have a range of different theories on hand to explain the same phenomena. At other times they mean that knowledge-producing communities should employ as many different methodologies as possible when engaged in their practices. Diversity can also mean that any single knowledge-producing community should contain as much cultural diversity as it possibly can. Diversity is also sometimes used to mean that a community should avoid exclusively generating the questions that it chooses to investigate from within its own walls. Rather, it should go outside to a diverse range of social groups to ask them what kinds of issues they think are important to investigate. It is not important in the current context to specify any one of these as the most important kind of diversity in epistemology. All of the different kinds can be made to support the argument to preserve a diversity of places. Evidence to show that diversity in general is important for knowledge is all that is needed to support the policy recommendation to preserve a diversity of natural places for epistemological reasons.

THE PHILOSOPHY OF SCIENCE ARGUMENT FOR DIVERSITY

A good place to start is with philosopher of science Paul K. Feyerabend's arguments for encouraging a proliferation of theories. The reputation that Feyerabend richly deserved as a leading twentieth-century philosopher of science is usually torpedoed by his status as a maverick and jokester. His outspoken challenges to the value of rationality in *Against Method* and *Farewell to Reason* make him an iconoclast among the philosophical community. Any philosopher who irreverently enjoins colleagues to bid farewell to their primary tool is unlikely to be appreciated. It has been hard for many philosophers to take seriously the opinions of a colleague who argued at length for the position that "there is no need to suppress even the most outlandish product of the human brain."[2] Despite his self-appointed role as a provocateur, Feyerabend made a compelling case for the importance of diversity to science.

Feyerabend acknowledged that his views on the importance of diversity owed much to his appreciation for the nineteenth-century British political reformer John Stuart Mill. Mill proposed several arguments in favor of a principle of proliferation in science. In an unselfconscious moment of Euroboosterism, Mill had proclaimed that the proliferation of viewpoints emanating from the large diversity of peoples in Europe was the main reason for the continent's "progressive and many sided development."[3] Proliferation was methodologically important, according to Mill, to compensate for human fallibility. "We can never be sure," said Mill, "that the opinion we are endeavoring to stifle is a false opinion" (16). Mill spelled out in some detail four particular reasons for not suppressing divergent opinions: (1) opinions one has reason to reject may yet turn out to be true; (2) rejected beliefs may contain elements of truth useful for plugging the gaps in an accepted theory; (3) prevailing beliefs that lack challengers will come to be held as a matter of prejudice with little attention to how well they account for the phenomena; (4) the full meaning of a prevailing belief can be realized only by contrast to the beliefs that it replaces and with which it is in competition.[4]

There was admittedly a lot of historical and philosophical space separating Mill from Feyerabend. By Feyerabend's time, many philosophers of science were considerably more skeptical of some of Mill's enlightenment ideas about science. Instead of retaining Mill's goal of absolute, one-time truths about the world, Feyerabend denied that knowledge should be regarded as a transcendent phenomenon, calling it instead "a local commodity designed to satisfy local needs and to solve local problems." Even some of the basic laws of nature were, in Feyerabend's eyes, local productions. "It needs a very special mental attitude," he said, "inserted into a particular social structure combined with sometimes quite idiosyncratic historical sequences to divine, formulate, check and establish laws such as the second law of thermodynamics."[5] It was a theoretical point about this localness that made Feyerabend support a radical version of Mill's principle of proliferation.

Feyerabend first observed that "one and the same set of observational data is compatible with very different and mutually inconsistent theories."[6] Theories are underdetermined by data, which often makes it hard to find evidence that can unequivocally allow a scientist to decide in favor of one theory rather than another. What makes this problem doubly difficult is that the theory dependence of observation thesis ensures that all empirical evidence is inevitably gathered against the background of a particular theoretical account of the world. Scientists always need to make at least some theoretical commitments even before they have gathered crucial evidence for or against a theory. Feyerabend used his knowledge of particular episodes in the history of science to suggest that sometimes the particular evidence needed to decide about a theory "[could] not be unearthed except with the help of alternatives to the theory being tested."[7] Alternative theoretical perspectives were in these cases required to bring determinative facts to light. Feyerabend claimed that this had been the case when it was necessary for Einstein's experiments with kinetic theory to determine that Brownian motion, and not the second law of thermodynamics, accurately characterized the motion of a small particle. The best way to proceed in science, Feyerabend concluded, was to collect observations relative to "a whole set of partly overlapping, factually adequate, but mutually inconsistent theories."[8] Only with such a profusion of different theories and evidence to hand would a scientist have enough data to make determinative judgments between theories. Science should strive, then, not to be monolithic but to be as theoretically diverse as time and money allow.

These arguments for proliferation allowed Feyerabend to incorporate much of what he had admired in Mill. Like Mill, Feyerabend recommended that empiricists "invent, and elaborate theories which are inconsistent with the accepted point of view, even if the latter should happen to be highly confirmed and generally accepted."[9] The invention of alternatives required that scientists learn to tolerate both competing theories and competing methods. Feyerabend's openness to radical alternatives was quite startling. "There is no idea, however ancient and absurd, that is not capable of improving our knowledge."[10] He painted a complex, dynamic, and mildly chaotic picture of the knowledge process. The only guideline that Feyerabend allowed was the iconoclastic "anything goes." The best way to avoid stagnation in science was to make diversity and proliferation of theories central. It soon becomes clear how Feyerabend's argument for theoretical and methodological diversity, once it has been connected to the grounding of knowledge, can be used to support the preservation of a diversity of places. Before that, I provide some more support for diversity in knowledge projects.

THE SOCIOLOGY OF SCIENCE ARGUMENT FOR DIVERSITY

Feyerabend's arguments for diversity are echoed by a different set of arguments articulated by feminists eager to avoid the masculinist values that permeate science. Most of these feminist arguments use as their starting point the sociological critiques of science described in chapter 2. Those critiques warned against the value biases that can sneak into scientific practice. Lorraine Code recommended taking subjectivity into account, and Sandra Harding recommended practicing strong objectivity.[11] Both are made necessary by the fact that "the lives from which thought has started are always present and visible in the results of that thought."[12] This means opening up the person or the group making the claim to some of the same kinds of scrutiny as the claim that they are putting forward.

It should be apparent from previous chapters that subjectivity in science can be both a good and a bad thing. Nazi science is undesirable. Public interest science is, presumably, desirable. Making these judgment calls is not always going to be easy, but it is clear that, with values slipping into science all the time, they are judgment calls that often have to be made. Donna Haraway has shown how it is possible not to despair about this and to put these subjectivities to good use. The inevitable partiality of knowledge claims, she asserts, makes objectivity into a matter of "limited location and situated knowledge, not about transcendence and splitting of subject and object. It allows us to become answerable for what we learn how to see."[13] Partiality can therefore be positive if it is used to encourage responsible knowledge claims—claims for which the claimant can be held accountable. Feminist standpoint theorists are even more positive about partiality and specifically seek out some biases they think are better than others. Standpoint theorists believe that the best kinds of biases are those brought by groups traditionally oppressed and left out of the business of producing knowledge by the dominant group. Only from this kind of lived, subordinated standpoint is it possible to offer "the most trenchant critiques of the dominant institutions and their discourse."[14] The methodological norm that follows from this is to start scientific research from questions generated in the social margins and to take those critiques of the mainstream institutions of knowledge production to be the most incisive. Both Haraway's and the standpoint theorist's discussions illustrate that it is possible to turn the presence of subjective values in knowledge into something useful. This was what Harding described as turning a prison house into a toolbox.

While subjectivity in a knowledge claim can be good or bad, one thing that is *always* bad is a subjectivity that remains hidden. All of the feminist approaches share a commitment to identifying values that are being introduced surreptitiously. This is the point at which the second argument for diversity begins. For knowledge-producing communities interested in spotting hidden values, diversity becomes a key tool. The more homogeneous a community is, the more widely distributed a particular bias is likely to be. The more widely distributed the bias is, the less likely it is to be visible to those who share it. In order to avoid this invisibility of biases, it is methodologically important to always ensure that the chosen methods and practices of those in charge of producing knowledge remain open to the criticism of those less likely to share all of the dominant cultural values. Some things can be seen only from the outside. Social and cultural diversity is therefore of great importance for the production of critical knowledge. It was the same kind of thinking that led Feyerabend to propose that "individuals, groups, and entire civilizations may profit from studying alien cultures, institutions, ideas, no matter how strong the arguments that support their own views."[15]

In order to foster this kind of diversity, knowledge-producing communities must be structured in ways that facilitate a diversity of participation and of criticism. Feyerabend asked for a free society in which an open exchange of views between specialists and nonspecialists is actively encouraged.[16] Feminist philosopher of science Helen Longino has argued for the construction of interactive, dialogic communities that are set up so that groups with different value biases can engage with each other. She offers the following four criteria as necessary to create the needed engagement:

1   There must be publicly recognized forums for the criticism of evidence, of methods, and of assumptions and reasoning.
2   The community must not merely tolerate dissent, but its beliefs and theories must change over time in response to the critical discourse taking place within it.
3   There must be publicly recognized standards by reference to which theories, hypotheses, and observational practices are evaluated and by appeal to which criticism is made relevant to the goal of the inquiring community. With the possible exception of empirical adequacy, there needn't be (and probably isn't) a set of standards common to all communities.
4   Finally, communities must be characterized by equality of intellectual authority. What consensus exists must not be the result of the exercise of political or economic power or the exclusion of dissenting perspectives; it must be the result of critical dialogue in which all the relevant perspectives are represented.[17]

Longino makes it clear that good science requires not just good scientists but also good communities. Communities must be set up in ways that leave open clear avenues for criticism and debate. Open avenues for debate ensure that a diversity of perspectives can always be brought to bear on knowledge production. These social arrangements are a way of countering what would otherwise be a harmful homogeneity in a knowledge community. The fact that everyone makes their knowledge claims from a particular social location means that it is important to place a high value on openness and diversity of opinion in the communities that we entrust with the production of knowledge. Longino envisions institutionalized arrangements to promote this diversity.

The Naturalistic Argument for Diversity

The two arguments for diversity from the philosophy of science and from the sociology of science follow a similar pattern. Both argue that seeking out differing perspectives—in the one case the perspective offered from a theoretical context and in the other the perspective offered from a social context—is important for the integrity of the knowledge process. To use the distinction employed in chapter 2, these are culturally rather than scientifically based arguments. An argument for diversity from the natural sciences would have to take a slightly different form. It would have to provide empirical evidence that diversity somehow contributes positively to the way the brain operates when it creates knowledge. A naturalistic argument in support of diversity would have to show that diversity is literally good for the functioning of the mind. It is interesting to note that Feyerabend had hoped that such an argument might one day be available to support his arguments for theoretical diversity in science. He complained that naturalistic explanations were "sorely underdiscussed" in the philosophy of science and speculated that certain modes of thinking might one day be discovered to be "physiologically more basic and are hence more firmly ingrained into human life, behavior and perception."[18] He hoped that cognitive science might eventually produce these results.

Though Feyerabend made these suggestions over a quarter of a century ago, it is not entirely clear that cognitive science is quite ready to fulfill his hope. It is still a considerable challenge to say much about how thought works at all, let alone to make helpful suggestions about what an individual or a community can do to make it work better. It is for good reason that although such cultural naturalizers as Feyerabend and Longino have often recommended creating particular social arrangements, few scientific naturalizers have made similar recommendations on the basis of their scientific understanding of cognition.[19] But even though arguments for particular epistemic norms have not often been made by scientific naturalizers, such arguments are fast becoming more plausible. It is especially suggestive for the purposes of this book that a naturalistic argument for diversity can be made based on Mark Johnson's account of the embodied mind.

Since he is neither a philosopher of science nor an epistemologist, Johnson does not spend a great deal of time making recommendations about how we should go about forming our beliefs and theories. But he does make a few remarks about the implications of his view for scientific objectivity, and these remarks suggest a few normative recommendations for epistemology. Johnson states that he wants to hold onto the notion of objectivity in his enactivist cognitive science on the condition that it is transformed into a human, rather than a God's eye, version. The human version of objectivity seeks to be accommodating of the fact that different people see things differently, while also recognizing that there are some important social and structural commonalities between different people. "It doesn't really matter," Johnson claims, "that we can't see the world through God's Eyes; for we can see the world through shared, public eyes that are given to us by our embodiment, our history, our culture, our language, our institutions, etc."[20] Sounding much like some of the sociologists of science already discussed, Johnson goes on to claim that objectivity is a matter of using different epistemic locations to critique publicly held viewpoints. Human objectivity is a process, he says, one of being "able to take up multiple perspectives as a way of both criticizing and transforming our own views and those of others."[21] Imaginatively taking up other perspectives is an essential part of the transformation and improvement of one's own views. This version of objectivity is what Stephen Winter has called "transperspectivity," or "an exercise of the empathetic ability to imagine what a question looks like from more than one side." Transperspectivity involves taking up the perspective of others and using it as a resource for "chang[ing] one's world in the light of possibilities revealed by those alternative viewpoints."[22] So far Johnson's account of embodied objectivity adds nothing that Feyerabend, Haraway, and Harding have not already said.

Yet hiding within what sounds like a familiar sociological account is a set of commitments reflecting something about how it is that the embodied mind actually works physiologically. According to Johnson, imaginatively taking up the perspective of others is more than just a generous empathetic gesture. It involves a particular operation of the embodied cognitive structures that underlie cognition. In chapter 2 it was explained how Johnson's account of cognition relies upon embodied patterns or schemas that help us make sense of experience and give structure to our beliefs. Such a view requires that we possess the ability to deploy these schemas in the face of experiences that are rarely, if ever, the same. There will also be occasions on which schemas will need to be transformed in order to remain useful. The part of us that makes these transformations possible is the "embodied imagination."

Taking his lead from Kant, Johnson claims that the imagination has both a schematizing and a creative function. In the former, it mediates between the schemas brought to experience and the data presented in experience, matching relatively stable and embodied structures to our constantly changing experience. In the latter function, the imagination transforms currently held sets of embodied cognitive structures to create new structures that will better fit experience. This technical understanding of the embodied imagination makes it into a crucial tool for making our cognitive way in the world. Embodied imagination is responsible for "our capacity to organize mental representations (especially percepts, images, and image schemata) into meaningful, coherent unities. It includes our ability to generate novel order."[23] The imagination is therefore the linchpin of Johnson's account of the embodied mind. Without it, no growth in meaning or understanding would be possible.

It is crucial that the imagination stays active and does its job well if knowledge is to progress. Image schemas are multiple, and creating meaning involves employing as many of them as possible. According to Johnson, there are "many other as-yet-unexplored schemes that will prove even more useful in pursuing our purposes as they are currently shaped" (209). It is the creative imagination that makes transperspectivity possible, and it is transperspectivity that makes progress possible. Exactly how the imagination manages to affect these transformations is unclear. It would be extraordinarily difficult to explain how something that is materially embodied in neurons and cell processes could also be continually at work creatively combining and recombining our existing schemas with our new experiences. These details are currently elusive and will likely remain so for some time to come. Yet plainly the imagination *can* do this work because without it we would be incapable of making sense of our lives. We would be unable to suggest new interpretations of events and to create new theories to account for novel experiences. As individuals and as cultures, without the operation of the embodied imagination we would remain stuck at the same level of understanding, unable to learn how to see things in different and better ways.

Even without knowing exactly how it works, it is clear that we should learn how to employ the embodied imagination as often and as broadly as possible if we want to increase the meaning of our experience and our understanding of the world. John Stuart Mill suggested that "the mental and the moral, like the muscular powers, improve only by being used." [24] If this is true of the creative imagination, then only by engaging with as many diverse opportunities as possible for the creative imagination to be active can humans hope to broaden their understanding of their place in the world. Without engaging in these activities, the creative imagination falls dangerously idle. Johnson therefore encourages us to "use as many of these imaginative methods as we can . . . transperspectivity requires it, for that is the only way we can criticize our present [moral] understanding . . . and expand our sense for the possibilities of constructive action." [25]

Johnson's view of the organism having to constantly reshape its schemas in order to increase the understanding of its experience belongs firmly in the American pragmatist tradition of John Dewey. Dewey characterized animate organisms as creatures that rely on habits to enable them to cope with experience. Dewey's habits are functionally similar to Johnson's schemas. Dewey saw humans as naturally habit-forming creatures and felt that our tendency is "towards monotonous regularity . . . [that] makes subsequent learning more difficult." He thought the way to counter this monotony was through continuous and diverse democratic communication. Communication, said Dewey, "not only increases the number and variety of habits, but tends to link them subtly together . . . thus habit is formed in view of possible future changes and does not harden so readily." Johnson's need to employ the creative imagination echoes Dewey's emphasis on the importance of the power of forming and re-forming habits. This power is something to be encouraged. Dewey observed how "increased power of forming habits means increased susceptibility, sensitiveness, responsiveness. Thus even if we think of habits as so many grooves, the power to acquire many and varied grooves denotes high sensitivity, explosiveness . . . [A]n old habit, a fixed groove . . . gets in the way of the process of forming a new habit while the tendency to form a new one cuts across some old habit."[26]

The power to acquire many and varied grooves is a power that Johnson claims resides in the embodied imagination. An organism's need to continually increase the meaning of its experience through acts of the creative imagination demands that a diversity of theories and perspectives be encouraged at all times. Seeking to understand a diversity of theories puts exactly the kind of demands on the creative imagination that are required if our understanding is not to stagnate. Theoretical and cultural diversity is the most reliable source of these demands. Taking theoretical and cultural diversity seriously means genuinely seeking to understand why things look different from different theoretical and cultural locations.

DIVERSITY AND PLACE

With these three arguments for the importance of diversity to the production of knowledge in hand, the stage is set to turn now to how this might support a policy recommendation for the preservation of a diversity of physical environments. The support emerges when these arguments for diversity are set alongside the connections I have been articulating between place and mind. In each of the three arguments for diversity, it was, to put it crudely, the benefits of getting one's head around something different that made diversity epistemically desirable. If this is the case, then factors that are capable of generating difference become extremely important resources for supporting critical knowledge practices. Existing epistemologies offer race, gender, ethnicity, and social class among the locations most often credited as reliable sources of difference. Sexuality, religion, age, and political allegiance can quickly be added as sources that might also play such a positive role. We can now begin to appreciate how place is also an important source of epistemically valuable diversity. As Harding pointed out, location in heterogeneous nature exposes people to different kinds of regularities that influence the things they think are important. Dramatic environmental differences lead to the elevation of the importance of some values over others. Harding wondered about the influence of living on a geological fault line. We might also wonder about the kinds of priorities adopted by those who live near eroding beaches or on a floodplain. Fishermen, firewood gatherers, automotive workers, ski patrollers, and those living at the bottom of deep canyons all interact with physical environments in ways that may influence their values and how they prioritize them. Sometimes these geographical influences are at least as important or may even exceed the importance of social influences such as gender, race, and social class. And at other times they no doubt are much less significant.

The mention of the significance of cultural activities such as fishing and firewood gathering occurring in different environments should make it more clear than ever that social and geographical influences can rarely be entirely separated from each other. Social class will affect whether you are a tea picker or a plantation owner in the Kisii region of Kenya and will influence whether you live in a mansion in Aspen or in a double-wide trailer in "Cancer Alley" in Louisiana. Gender, sexuality, and race also continue to have considerable influence on the opportunities society makes available to a person. These social factors will affect how a person ends up interacting with his or her environment. But even if multiple social and natural factors interact in complex ways to yield a person's positionality in the world, it is important to be aware of the forces that are making up the mix. Physical environment is clearly one of the factors that is capable of generating diversity.

If cultural diversity is an important tool for helping to spot the biases that are creeping into knowledge claims, then the diversity of different physical environments, as a sponsor of cultural diversity, must also be such a tool. People living in diverse physical environments have the potential to bring insightful perspectives into the interactive, dialogic communities that Longino envisioned. This is going to be especially true of people who participate in daily activities that cause them to be in close contact with what is distinctive about those environments. So, for example, the perspectives of farmers in rural Iowa will be more distinctive of that geographic region than the perspectives of stockbrokers in Chicago. The perspectives of farmers have been achieved through their culture and their bodies. The soil of the Midwest has physically passed through the farmers' hands and influenced the muscular activities of their body. Diverse environments literally supply the physical material that is of cognitive importance. People who work on the land have more contact with a greater range of that physical material. These physical locations yield perspectives that can be used as toolboxes rather than regarded as prison houses for the knowledge process. Like other factors contributing to cultural diversity, a diversity of physical environments is a valuable source that helps to increase the number of perspectives available.[27]

The naturalistic argument for diversity works in largely similar ways. If it is indeed good for the way that our minds function to take up the theories and methodologies of diverse others, then the arguments used by Harding can be imported wholesale onto the ground that has been prepared by Johnson. If physical location in nature is one of the factors influencing the values we incorporate into our belief systems, then this location contributes something important when it comes time to keep the embodied imagination active. Physical environments contribute to generating those perspectives that Johnson argues are good for us to take up. Giving serious consideration to the belief systems and values of different peoples from different places will be part of what is required to keep the creative imagination agile. An agile embodied imagination is better able to increase the meaning of our experience. It staves off the monotonous regularity of habit that Dewey feared. As a factor that creates demand on the imagination, diverse physical environments should be highly valued.

But Johnson's naturalistic argument for diversity suggests that diverse places can also take a more direct role in keeping the imagination operating as effectively as it can. Diverse places do more than contribute to critical knowledge by generating diverse cultural perspectives. To see what else they can do we should recall the connections between sensorimotor and cognitive activity described earlier. In Johnson's embodied account, the schemas used in cognition are derivatives of the schemas used in sensorimotor activity. The balance schema is useful both for staying upright and for structuring concepts such as justice and mathematical equality. This connection between sensorimotor and cognitive schemas suggests an additional way that physical environments generate diversity. They generate a diversity of embodied sensorimotor schemas that might later prove to be useful for cognition. Walking long distances on snow, bundled up against the cold in Manitoba, requires significantly different embodied schemas from kayaking through the steamy swamps of the low country of South Carolina. What Dewey referred to as "the power to acquire many and varied grooves" is a power that diversity of physical environments encourages. This means that the way in which we move around diverse environments with our bodies is in itself *cognitively* significant.

To unpack this claim a bit further, I suggest that there are at least two reasons why creating multiple, fresh sets of sensorimotor schemas might be cognitively useful. First, any new embodied schema is a potentially useful tool for thought. Engaging with different physical geographies can generate resources in the form of embodied schemas that might later profitably be turned to cognitive use. Second, being adept at moving between different sensorimotor schemas hones a similar skill to the one that it takes to move deftly between different cognitive schemas. The same embodied imagination that allows us to generate new and appropriate schemas in situations that are physically challenging is also employed in creating new and appropriate schemas in situations that are cognitively challenging.

The closeness of this relationship between the tools we use in cognition and the tools we use in sensorimotor experience is indicated by the phenomenology of certain particularly challenging physical experiences. Many dramatic changes in physical environment require some significant degree of bodily adjustment. Take as an example the feeling of going out on the ocean in a small boat after being on land for an extended period. The first few hours on a boat usually cause a strange kind of disorientation often described colloquially as not yet having your sea legs. There is a kind of sensorimotor confusion that results from having to be very deliberate about when and where to put your feet down. Embodied schemas have to be learned or be deployed in patterns that have fallen into disuse. Often new patterns of bodily comportment have to be quickly generated. The interesting thing about this process is that it does not feel like a sensorimotor challenge alone. Those who have experienced the feeling of not having their sea legs typically find that the disorientation feels much broader than a simple bodily uncertainty. It actually feels like a low level of *cognitive* confusion in addition to the obvious *sensorimotor* confusion. There is something that is rather disturbing to the mind about not yet having your sea legs. "Things are not supposed to be like this. . . . I can usually make it across the room without staggering. . . . How did the back of that table arrive painfully in my ribs?" Even though a person might know exactly what is going on, the lack of sea legs always causes a bit of cognitive confusion. At the same time, it can also cause a trace of excitement at the possibilities opened up by an experience that is so different from normal and that demands so much creativity from the body.

Some of the same feelings arise during a ride at an amusement park. The unfamiliar forces that operate on the body in these situations are both alarming and thrilling, the result of the close relationship between sensorimotor and cognitive disorientation. The bodily reorientations that take place during a roller-coaster ride are both bodily and mentally confusing. The confusion can come in different degrees. Usually it is of pretty low level. But if the ride at the amusement park has been particularly good, the level of cognitive disorientation can be quite high. Sometimes even speaking coherently immediately after getting off a roller coaster can be a bit of a challenge. A person would certainly not want to take an important test of analytic skills immediately after the ride. People learn to enjoy this confusion and even to seek it out for entertainment, but the reorientations remain a significant challenge to both body and mind.

Johnson's naturalistic account of the embodied imagination explains why we should not be surprised that the feelings of sensorimotor disorientation and cognitive confusion so often merge together. They merge because they are both the feeling of the same embodied imagination working hard to pull up or create schemas appropriate for the novel situation. Existing schemas cannot fit every possible experience perfectly, and the embodied imagination can take a little while to find the right combinations to deploy. In certain situations, the embodied imagination will need to create some entirely new schemas in order to make experience meaningful. The feeling of confusion reflects the struggle of the embodied imagination to hastily rearrange sensorimotor and cognitive structure so that a person can feel at home in the new situation.

The closeness of this relationship between the sensorimotor and the cognitive would explain the feelings that I described experiencing shortly after I arrived in Dry Bay, Alaska. My embodied imagination had a lot on its plate on arrival. The dramatic landscape at Dry Bay provoked a little bit of consternation and more than a hint of excitement as I began my perceptual, motor, and cognitive adjustment. Like the sensorimotor problem of lacking sea legs, it often manifested itself in the form of low-level cognitive confusion. The feelings of confusion were the feelings of the embodied imagination hard at work. The confusion was operating both at the level of sensorimotor and of cognitive function. Dislocating experiences are therefore both literally and metaphorically dislocating. One suggestive corollary of this is that since dislocating experiences demand that the embodied imagination stay creative, they might actually be quite good for us under certain circumstances.[28]

THE PRESERVATION OF LANDSCAPE DIVERSITY

When the importance of diversity for critical knowledge has been set alongside the grounding of knowledge, a specific policy recommendation follows. Diverse natural landscapes and the communities that call them home must not be destroyed or homogenized through development. Landscape diversity is a valuable source of the diversity sought by epistemologists. Ensuring the preservation of both cultural and natural diversity is therefore important for ensuring the production of critical knowledge. The more that living in the

Front Range of the Rocky Mountains becomes like living in the desert around Phoenix, and the more that both of these become like living in Trenton, New Jersey, then the less guarantee that people will bring to the table helpful differences of perspective generated by the geographical locale in which they live. One of the important contributing factors toward the generation of diversity will have been erased. Sameness of landscapes breeds a sameness of mind. It should be no surprise that cultural diversity and biodiversity are so closely linked.

We should note again here that these arguments for diversity based on the connection of place and mind make it particularly important to preserve the insights of individuals and cultures that have spent a long period of time allowing the particularity of their place to seep into their structures of belief. Cognitive senses of place are not so easy to come by in highly mobile cultures. They should be highly valued where they are found. We should also note that according to this argument, diverse artifactual environments are also of cognitive and epistemic value. It is a good thing for knowledge production that there are some people whose sense of place is connected to San Francisco and others whose sense of place is connected to Normal, Illinois. Office towers and sprawling ranch houses each offer different environmental structures that the mind can use as a toolbox. It is a good thing *for the sake of cognitive diversity* that some people live in one-room shacks and others live in fourteen-bedroom mansions. The different environments have the potential to create different and valuable cognitive structures. Standpoint theorists persuasively argue that the perspective from the one-room shack is much more useful to society than the perspective from the mansion. Fortunately, none of these observations show that it is a good thing that our society fosters such disparity. The preservation of cognitive diversity is not the only guide for how we should organize society. Important social justice considerations will often overrule the benefits of different cognitive perspectives.

Even though natural and artifactual diversity are both important generators of cognitive diversity, it is possible to sketch a reason for taking special care to preserve a diversity of natural environments. Even without Shepard's evolutionary arguments, natural environments should be preserved because they provide some of the greatest sources of cognitive diversity. They supply some of the greatest ranges of textures, shapes, sights, and sounds of any kind of environment. Natural environments are inherently unpredictable, autonomous, and structurally dynamic. The environments and the organisms that populate them *actually do things.* They have a material and biological agency that always goes beyond what is created in the human realm. Pickering earlier asked us to "think of the weather" because there is a material agency in weather that is often more impressive than the material agency in the lab. This highlights how we continually have to adjust in the face of nature's agency when we move away from the artifactual. Within the human realm, by contrast, we rely heavily on architects and planners to make our artifactual environments diverse. We are forced into this dependence because the building materials out of which these environments are constructed, the economic considerations according to which they are planned, and the political structures that enable them to evolve (and us to evolve in them) continually pull these environments toward homogeneity rather than diversity. The ride into town from the airport looks much the same whether you are in Bangor, Maine, or Sacramento, California. The inside of an airplane or a car hardly changes from one side of the world to the other. Natural environments, on the other hand, have variability and unpredictability built into them. Even those natural environments that are not the most biologically diverse in terms of numbers of species often supply possibilities for experience that are hard to find elsewhere. Rainforests and ice caps should both be highly valued for the resources they offer the mind. The types of diversity that are characteristic of environments under less human control will always make them into particularly important sources of cognitive value. Their increasing rarity only elevates that value. Although humans can create epistemically desirable kinds of diversity on their own initiative, naturally occurring diversity remains a reliable and potent source of cognitive value. And it is a form of diversity that is rapidly being squandered. We have to be concerned about something of such high value that is being destroyed so carelessly.

The discussion has just touched down again on that tricky question of how to value cultural things relative to natural things. I earlier promised to revisit the tension that I warned would be running throughout the book. The first time it surfaced, this tension was about whether to give precedence to the cultural or to the scientific naturalizers. The next time it was about whether places are more culturally or naturally determined. In the previous chapter, it reappeared in the observation that cultural considerations influence how people interact with nature and then again in a heavily disguised form in the question of whether to value nature as an epistemic source intrinsically or instrumentally. Now it appears again over whether we should value the diversity of culturally constructed epistemic sources more or less than the diversity of naturally occurring sources.

I hope I have made it clear that there are good reasons to recognize the importance of both the products of culture and the products of nature. Each is a genuine source of multiple values. I hope I have also made it clear that it is not always possible to sustain a workable distinction between what belongs on the cultural side and what belongs on the natural side of the great divide in the first place. Part of the argument of this book has been that the criterion most often used to mark this distinction—the ability that humans have to use reason to create knowledge—is perhaps not as good a criterion as was previously thought. But having said this, it is important to add that in environmental philosophy there are dangers involved in not maintaining that the nonhuman side of the divide is particularly important to isolate and to emphasize. An inescapable background assumption in environmental philosophy is that it is nonhuman nature that is imperiled, not humanity. It is the world aside from humans that is being lost, not the world of humans. It is unlikely that contemporary caution over the problems involved in separating the cultural from the natural in any way alters the stark ecological reality. Nonhuman nature *is* being destroyed by humans. No amount of redefinition and rethinking of the human/nature divide can make that fact go away.

It is also important to focus on the nonhuman side of the division between culture and nature because the debate does not take place on a level playing field. As I have already mentioned a number of times, postmodern epistemology has up to this point been lamentably anthropocentric. Even those thinkers whom I have praised for starting to recognize that places count positively in the construction of knowledge have already made anthropocentric judgments about how to divide the relative weight between culture and nature. Harding puts the weight on culture, saying that the category of localness created by location in heterogeneous nature gains its value only through cultural practices.[29] She fails to fully acknowledge the value of the environment as the real source of epistemic localness. Harding's position echoes the one in Basso's description of the role of place in Western Apache morality. Basso stresses how the role of the place is contingent upon numerous cultural factors including the length of residence, the cultural activities practiced, and historical circumstance. Neither Harding nor Basso wants to suggest anything too deterministic about place. They recognize that cultural and natural influences are hard to keep apart, and they use this to justify their reluctance to ascribe too much agency to the natural influences alone.

But even if cultural and natural influences are hard to separate entirely from each other, I am concerned about how Harding and Basso have weighted things. I worry about the natural influences not being given enough significance. A different way to weight the emphasis would be to regard the natural environment itself, and not the culture living there, as a significant portion of the source of epistemic value. When Harding described location in hetero-geneous nature as one of the causes of indigenous knowledge practices, she quickly put the word "cause" into scare quotes to avoid accusations of being an environmental determinist. But what this brings to the fore is just how difficult it has become to talk about the physical aspects of nature in contem-porary epistemology. At several points in this book, I have pointed out that place and mind are in a dialectical relationship, continually and dynamically shaping each other. It is certainly the case that neither of the parties in a di-alectical relationship should be allowed to claim conceptual priority. But it is equally true that neither should be forced into disappearing from sight and losing its significance. As long as we live within an intellectual framework that remains largely anthropocentric, we can always expect that natural factors will be dropped out in favor of cultural ones. Environmentalists should be on their guard against this.

Not letting the physical environment drop out means never silencing na-ture and rendering it irrelevant to knowledge projects. Donna Haraway has professed an eagerness to treat nature "as an actor and an agent . . . not as a screen or a ground or a resource . . . never as a slave to the master that closes off the dialectic in his unique agency and authorship of knowledge."[30] Treat-ing nature as an actor and an agent is on Haraway's and my own terms an important part of the revisioning of the culture/nature dualism that is so of-ten blamed for environmentally destructive behavior patterns. Answering the question of exactly how much agency we are willing to ascribe to natural en-vironments relative to cultural environments will undoubtedly require more empirical studies of perception and cognition, more sociologies of science, and more human geography. These kinds of studies will be especially neces-sary for those who are only persuaded by the precise articulation of specific material causes. But for others, such studies can only provide additional evi-dence for what they already know about the marvelous potency of place and about the necessary connections between place and mind. In either case, Har-away's metaphor of nature as Coyote is helpful. Haraway calls Coyote "the coding trickster with whom we must learn to converse."[31] Coyote can be an important and whimsical reminder that nonhuman nature is always involved in our lives, somehow and somewhere, even when it comes to the innermost workings of the human mind.

Notes

Introduction

1 As the international space station floats 233 miles above our heads with its community of astronauts and cosmonauts, it is clear that this claim will not remain true indefinitely. The space station will allow humans to make knowledge claims from somewhere other than planet earth. However, even if astronauts, cosmonauts, and space tourists promise a future of creating knowledge fully detached from the earth, the abilities that they have to do this will for a long time remain learned and practiced here on earth. Only if there comes a time in which people are born and live their lives in space will the project of grounding knowledge have to take on additional dimensions.

2 Shepard, "Place in American Culture," 23.

3 Leopold, *Sand County Almanac,* 214.

4 Snyder, *Real Work*; Jackson, *Becoming Native.*

5 Allen, *Sacred Hoop.*

6 Basso, *Wisdom Sits in Places.*

7 Abram, *Spell of the Sensuous,* 265.

1 Unnatural Knowledge

1 Shepard, *Nature and Madness,* 7.

2 Plato, *Apology,* trans. H. Tredennick, in *Collected Dialogues of Plato,* 17a–c.

3 Plato, *Republic,* trans. P. Shorey, in, *Collected Dialogues of Plato,* 517b.

4 Plato, *Symposium,* 210a–b.

5 The use of the word "mind" to talk about Plato's and later Aristotle's views is anachronistic. Though the Greeks did have the notion of something rational and immaterial inside of us responsible for thinking, they lacked our familiar dualistic conception of mind and body as completely separate substances. This separation did not appear until Descartes's *Meditations* in the seventeenth century. I use the term "mind" a little sloppily here to stand in for the intellectual part of us that the Greeks thought was the vehicle for producing knowledge.

6 Plato, *Symposium,* 211a–b.

7 Plato, *Timaeus,* trans. B. Jowett, in *Collected Dialogues of Plato,* 27d–28a.

8 Plato, *Phaedrus,* 247c.

9 Plato, *Phaedo,* trans. by H. Tredennick, in *Collected Dialogues of Plato,* 67c–d.

10 Plato, *Phaedrus,* 249d.

11 Aristotle, *De Anima,* trans. J. A. Smith, in *Basic Works of Aristotle,* 429a15. I acknowledge here again that it is not technically correct to use the term "mind" for the part of us that gains knowledge in Aristotle. Better terminology would be "the rational part of the soul." See note 5 above.

12 Ibid., 429a24–25.

13 Ibid., 429a19–20.

14 Locke, *Essay Concerning Human Understanding*, 552.

15 Descartes, *Meditations*, in *Selected Philosophical Writings*.

16 Locke, *Essay Concerning Human Understanding*, 47.

17 Descartes, *Objections and Replies*, in *Selected Philosophical Writings*, 132.

18 These differences are elegantly explained by Richard Rorty in his *Philosophy and the Mirror of Nature*.

19 Descartes, *Meditations*, 89.

20 Locke, *Essay Concerning Human Understanding*, 391, 393.

21 Ibid., 118.

22 Descartes, *Meditations*, 76.

23 Hume, *Enquiry Concerning Human Understanding*, 153.

24 Hume, *Treatise of Human Nature*, 218.

25 See Rorty, *Philosophy and the Mirror of Nature*, 45–61.

26 Latour, *Pandora's Hope*, 4.

27 Ewing, *Short Commentary*, 71.

28 Schlick, "Foundation of Knowledge," 247.

29 Quine, "Epistemology Naturalized," in *Ontological Relativity*, 72.

30 Ibid.

31 Quine, *Roots of Reference*, 2.

32 Quine, "Epistemology Naturalized," 82.

33 Latour, *Pandora's Hope*, 5.

34 Quine, "Epistemology Naturalized," 78.

2 Grounding Knowledge

1 It is interesting to note that of the two, Kant seemed more interested in geography, lecturing regularly on the topic at Königsberg University. See Burch, "Ethical Determination of Geography."

2 As the next few sections indicate, I use the term "naturalized epistemology" to stand for something considerably broader than the traditional usage.

3 An example of a collection of work that does take this approach seriously is Giere, *Cognitive Models of Science*.

4 The following section is informed by Francisco Varela, Evan Thompson, and Eleanor Rosch's survey of contemporary approaches to cognitive science. See Varela, Thompson and Rosch, *Embodied Mind*.

5 Ibid., 140.

6 Rorty, *Truth and Progress*, 20.

7 Varela, Thompson, and Rosch, *Embodied Mind*, 172–173.

8 Piaget and Beth, *Mathematical Epistemology*, 196.

9 Hesse and Arbib, *Construction of Reality*.

10 Hesse, "Need a Constructed Reality," 52.

11 Hess and Arbib, *Construction of Reality*, 45.

12 Johnson, *Body in the Mind*.

13 Ibid., xiv.

14 This is a difficult argument to make, and what follows is the barest sketch of it. For more details see Johnson, *Body in the Mind*; Johnson, *Moral Imagination*; and Lakoff and Johnson, *Philosophy in the Flesh*.

15 Just how a schema gets extended to other domains—through metaphor—is a major part of Johnson's book.

16 Lakoff and Johnson, *Philosophy in the Flesh*, 20.

17 Code borrows this phrase from Annette Baier. See Code, "What Is Natural?" 8.

18 Hayles, "Searching for Common Ground," 49.

19 This suggestion is discussed in more detail later in the book.

20 Johnson, *Body in the Mind*, xv–xvi.

21 Zilman, "Gathering Stories."

22 Russet, *Sexual Science*; Gould, *Mismeasure of Man*; Proctor, *Racial Hygiene*; Stephan, *Idea of Race in Science*.

23 Code, "Taking Subjectivity into Account."

24 Cited in Code, *What Can She Know?* 170.

25 Harding, "Rethinking Standpoint Epistemology," 69.

26 Code, "Taking Subjectivity into Account," 20.

27 Harding, *Science Question in Feminism*.

28 Pickering, *Mangle of Practice*, 9.

29 Ibid., 10.

30 This distinction was first made in Hacking, *Representing and Intervening*.

31 Knorr-Cetina, "Laboratory Studies," 116.

32 Ibid., 134.

33 Pickering, *Mangle of Practice*, 6. This is an insight that I soon request we take outside of the laboratory.

34 Haraway, *Simians, Cyborgs, and Women*.

35 Knorr-Cetina, "Couch, Cathedral, and Laboratory," 115.

36 The tangle also involves other mixes of the scientific and the cultural approaches. Steve Fuller, for example, explores the possibility that "both social and cognitive factors can profitably be retained in science studies." See Shadish and Fuller, *Social Psychology of Science*, 6–7.

37 Code, "What Is Natural?" 7.

38 Latour, "Give Me a Laboratory," 154.

39 Knorr-Cetina, "Laboratory Studies," 163.

40 Hutchins, *Cognition in the Wild*.

41 Knorr-Cetina, "Couch, Cathedral, and Laboratory," 116 n. 7.

42 Pickering, *Mangle of Practice*, 6.

3 Organisms and Environments

1 Slovic, "Nature Writing and Environmental Psychology," 351.

2 Hutchins, *Cognition in the Wild,* xiv.

3 See Bruno Latour's interesting interchange with a scientist that is related in the beginning of *Pandora's Hope.*

4 Varela, Thompson, and Rosch, *Embodied Mind,* 140.

5 Levins and Lewontin, *Dialectical Biologist,* 97.

6 Lewontin, *Biology as Ideology,* 26.

7 Levins and Lewontin, *Dialectical Biologist,* 89.

8 Varela, Thompson, and Rosch, *Embodied Mind,* 194.

9 Johnson, *Body in the Mind,* 137.

10 Varela, Thompson, and Rosch outline some of this work in chapter 9 of *Embodied Mind.*

11 Gibson, *Ecological Approach to Visual Perception.*

12 This is how Gibsonian Edward S. Reed characterizes the dilemma in *Encountering the World,* 6.

13 This can be accurately described as a reconnection because, prior to Descartes, the Greek view already included this link.

14 Gibson, *Perception of the Visual World.*

15 Gibson, *Ecological Approach,* 1.

16 Notice the parallels between Gibson's insight and Quine's. In light of the difficulties of finding out what is going on beneath the skin of the thinking and perceiving organism, each theorist came to see those internal mysteries as integrally linked to interactions taking place between the organism and its environment.

17 Gibson, *Ecological Approach,* 53.

18 Reed and Jones, "James Gibson's Ecological Revolution in Psychology," 91.

19 Gibson, *Ecological Approach,* 8.

20 There are a number of decidedly Kantian aspects of this view. For further discussion see Ben-Zeev, "Kantian Revolution in Perception."

21 With so much emphasis on sensorimotor action, Ben-Zeev complains about how Gibsonians "have not realized the opportunities afforded to their own approach by the notion of a schema" (79). He suggests that schemas can help explain how an organism picks up the affordances offered by the environment. See Ben-Zeev, "Kantian Revolution in Perception."

22 Reed, *James J. Gibson,* 235.

23 Gibson, *Ecological Approach.* Since plants are not considered animate, Gibson does not believe that the study of perception can be extended to include plants. However, to the extent that plants keep in touch with their world by sending out roots to seek water, by orienting themselves in relation to gravity, and by turning their leaves toward the sun to assist in photosynthesis, they certainly act in response to what their environment affords. This suggests that, in the Gibsonian view, it makes

sense to talk of plants as perceiving. Moreover, this conclusion seems to support a desirable gradualism among the biota. See Reed and Jones, "Gibson's Theory of Perception," 526–527 n. 4, for a short discussion of perception in plants.

24 Gibson, *Ecological Approach*, 129.
25 Ben-Zeev, "Kantian Revolution in Perception," 80.
26 Mace, "James J. Gibson's Strategy for Perceiving."
27 Rowlands, *Body in Mind.*
28 Gibson, *Ecological Approach*, 258.
29 See Reed, *James J. Gibson*, chapter 16.
30 Reed, *Encountering the World*, 82.
31 Varela, Thompson, and Rosch, *Embodied Mind*, 173.
32 Held and Hein, "Adaptation of Disarranged Hand-Eye Coordination."
33 Rosch, "Principles of Categorization."
34 Gibson, *Ecological Approach*, 8.
35 Rowlands, *Body in Mind.*
36 Putnam, "Meaning and Reference." See also Burge, "Individualism and the Mental."
37 Rowlands, *Environmental Crisis*, 96.
38 Rowlands, *Body in Mind*, chapter 3.
39 Clark, "Where Brain, Body, and World Collide," 264.
40 Ibid., 260.
41 Shepard, "On Animal Friends," 279.
42 Roszak, Gomes, and Kanner, *Ecopsychology.*
43 Johnson, *Body in the Mind*, 207.
44 Ibid.
45 Casey, *Fate of Place.*

4 Active Landscapes

1 Abram, *Spell of the Sensuous*, 217.
2 Quoted in Church, *Bacon*, 67.
3 The description of knowledge production as taking place "in the thick of things" is one now regularly used by Andrew Pickering.
4 This distinction between space and place has been articulated by Yi-Fu Tuan in *Space and Place*. Places have a particularity, familiarity, and agency in our lives that spaces, which are merely geometrically bounded areas, lack. In *Getting Back into Place*, Edward S. Casey characterizes this as the distinction between "place" and "site."
5 Tuan, *Space and Place*, 4.
6 Environmental philosophy in North America has been going through a number of stimulating debates about the coherence of notions such as "wilderness" and "natural." It is clear that early environmental philosophy somehow forgot to rec-

ognize that the North American continent was not an untamed wilderness when Columbus arrived. See Callicott and Nelson, *Great New Wilderness Debate.*

7 Plato, *Timaeus,* trans. Benjamin Jowett, in Plato, *Collected Dialogues,* 52b.

8 Casey, *Fate of Place,* 39.

9 Plato, *Phaedrus.*

10 Plato, *Phaedrus,* xliv.

11 Casey, *Fate of Place; Getting Back into Place;* and "How to Get from Space to Place."

12 Casey, *Fate of Place,* 333.

13 Jenness, *Ojibwa Indians of Parry Island.*

14 See, for example, Booth and Jacobs, "Ties That Bind"; and Callicott, "Traditional American Indian and Western Attitudes."

15 Deloria, *Custer Died for Your Sins,* chapter 4.

16 See much of Deloria's work and also the powerful criticism of environmental ethicists made in Cordova, "Eco-Indian."

17 Over the last few years I have learned some hard lessons about the complexity and difficulty of bringing Native American views into non-Native environmental ethics. Jim Cheney, through his own excellent work, has done more than anyone else to reassure me that it can be done in a sensitive fashion. In "Rivers of Thought," a paper given at the Aboriginal People's Conference at Lakehead University in Ontario, Cheney suggested "delving into resonating indigenous ideas, ideas that don't come with the baggage of Euro-American subtexts . . . has the real potential for reworking the Euro-American ideas in fruitful ways . . . [b]ut (and this is the important part) it isn't the sameness of the resonating ideas that matters (such as it is) . . . rather it is the differences that are the most exciting."

18 Basso, *Wisdom Sits in Places.*

19 Abram, *Spell of the Sensuous,* 162.

20 Ibid.

21 Basso, "Stalking with Stories," 95.

22 Basso, *Wisdom Sits in Places,* 143.

23 Deloria, *God Is Red.* As a Sioux Indian, Deloria perhaps possesses more authority than non-Indian commentators to make the generalizations he does.

24 Aristotle, *Physics,* trans. R. P. Hardie and R. K. Gaye, in Aristotle, *Basic Works,* 208B34.

25 Greta Gaard has made some similar observations about what happens when we enter wilderness areas in "Ecofeminism and Wilderness." Gaard claims that the altered relationship into which we enter in these different places gives us particular tools for thinking about how nature and culture interact.

26 I learned this powerful term from my friend Paul Fletcher, who was using it in a different context.

27 Portions of this narrative have been previously published in abbreviated form in my "Environment and Belief: The Importance of Place in the Construction of Knowledge."

28 Muir, *Wilderness Journeys*, 104.

29 Perhaps the best source for this history is DeLaguna, *Under Mount Saint Elias*.

30 This phenomenon of learning how to sense in a new place also became evident to me through working on fishing boats in Alaska. Most boats keep the VHF radio on all the time. At first it was an annoying intrusion into the auditory space, but after a while I learned how to tune it out into the background so that I hardly heard it. However, when a voice on the radio would announce "Pan-pan . . . Pan-pan . . . Pan-pan" (a call for attention) or "F/V Reflection" (the name of my boat), the sound would leap out of the background into the center of my attention. Like everything that I have been saying about perception so far, this sensitivity to certain sounds on the radio was a product of the kind of activities in which I was engaged (commercial fishing) and the nature of the physical environment in which I was acting (a cold sea).

31 Gaard, "Ecofeminism and Wilderness," 17.

32 Tuan, *Topophilia*, chapter 7.

33 Hanson, *Patterns of Discovery*.

34 Miles and Wallman, *Visual Motion*.

35 Tuan, *Topophilia*, 75–91.

5 Making Place Matter

1 Rehmann-Sutter, "Genes in Labs."

2 Admittedly, there remains the possibility that Nazi science, racist as it was, might yet by some criteria still have been "good" science. This is not an issue I attempt to resolve here. I think it is still safe to say that even if Nazi science was good science according to certain limited criteria, it is still not the sort of science that we want.

3 There is obviously a worry here that this search for hidden subjectivities could become absurd. I cannot imagine it being a good thing to investigate whether having long rather than short hair introduces a value bias. But within limits, openness to possible sources of distortion seems like a sensible precaution.

4 Borgmann, *Crossing the Post-Modern Divide*.

5 Cheney, "Post-Modern Environmental Ethics," 119.

6 Bigwood, *Earth Muse*, 43.

7 Mann, "World Alienation in Feminist Thought."

8 Tuana, "Material Locations."

9 Harding, *Is Science Multicultural?*, chapter 4. Harding does not label them "super-categories." This is my own term.

10 Donna Haraway also stands out among feminist epistemologists for the work she has done explaining how a partial perspective does not mean a limited perspective. See Haraway, "Situated Knowledges."

11 I have more to say about this in chapter 6.

12 Mark Rowland's *Environmental Crisis* is a rare and exciting example of a work that does make some of these connections.

13 Aristotle, *Nicomachean Ethics,* trans. W. D. Ross, in *Basic Works of Aristotle,* 1098a8.

14 Warren, "Power and Promise."

15 See, for example, Allen and Beckoff, *Species of Mind.*

16 Dennett, *Darwin's Dangerous Idea,* 371.

17 Rowlands has already brought some of these implications to bear on specific debates in environmental ethics. He uses his environmentalist model of cognition to review the distinction between valuing nature intrinsically and valuing it instrumentally. See Rowlands, *Environmental Crisis.*

18 See Rolston, *Environmental Ethics* and *Conserving Natural Value.*

19 Rolston, *Environmental Ethics,* 3.

20 Johnson, *Body in the Mind,* xv–xvi.

21 Rolston, *Environmental Ethics,* 9.

22 Rolston, "Why Species Matter," 508.

6 Preserving Place and Mind

1 As was pointed out at the end of the last chapter, a diversity of places modified by humans is likewise desirable. Small towns, urban jungles, and scattered trailer parks will make similar contributions to cognitive architecture as long as these artifactual places are not homogenized.

2 Feyerabend, *Philosophical Papers,* 1:143.

3 Mill, *On Liberty,* 69. "Progressive" is perhaps an unfortunate choice of word to describe nations regularly engaged in such imperialistic and exploitative endeavors.

4 Mill, *On Liberty,* 50–51.

5 Feyerabend, *Farewell to Reason,* 28, 88.

6 Feyerabend, *Philosophical Papers,* 1:59.

7 Ibid.

8 Feyerabend, *Against Method,* 27.

9 Feyerabend, *Philosophical Papers,* 1:105.

10 Feyerabend, *Against Method,* 33.

11 Code, "Taking Subjectivity into Account"; Harding, *Science Question in Feminism.*

12 Harding, "Rethinking Standpoint Epistemology," 63.

13 Haraway, "Situated Knowledges," 583.

14 Harding, *Is Science Multicultural?,* 142.

15 Feyerabend, *Farewell to Reason,* 20.

16 Feyerabend, *Science in a Free Society.*

17 Longino, "Subjects, Power, and Knowledge," 112–113.

18 Feyerabend, *Farewell to Reason,* 131.

19 Paul Churchland is an exception to this. He brings evidence from neurobiology to support some central Feyerabendian themes including his emphasis on the impor-

tance of diversity to cognition. See Churchland, "Deeper Unity" and "To Transform the Phenomena"; for some similar approaches, see other articles in Giere's *Cognitive Models in Science*. See also Nersessian, "Cognitive-Historical Approach"; Thagard, *Computational Philosophy of Science*; and Fuller and Shadish, *Social Psychology of Science*.

20 Johnson, *Body in the Mind*, 211.

21 Johnson, *Moral Imagination*, 241.

22 Ibid.

23 Johnson, *Body in the Mind*, 140.

24 Mill, *On Liberty*, 56.

25 Johnson, *Moral Imagination*, 242.

26 All Dewey quotations are taken from Dewey, *Experience and Nature*, 280–281.

27 This is a good moment to remember that diverse artifactual environments such as cities and concrete landscapes will also be sources of different perspectives. In the urban environment, a concern might arise that the recommendation to preserve diverse environments might be used to suggest preserving certain slums and ghettos so that society might gain cognitively from the unique physical structures that surround the people who live there. What this illustrates is that the obligation to preserve physical environments for cognitive gain must be defeasible in the face of certain other social goods (see p. 133).

28 This suggests that another way to keep the imagination active at an individual level might be to embrace as many different varieties of sensorimotor encounters as we can. Making our way through different kinds of activities in different kinds of environments will demand of our embodied imagination a helpful kind of agility. This agility can be helpful not only to prevent us from falling over when onboard boats but also to help ensure that we are always cognitively flexible. For the embodied mind, being good at thinking is often related to being good at being embodied. Diverse physical environments can be an important stimulus for the part of us that is crucial for effective cognition. But these are speculations that admit many exceptions. As such they should be treated cautiously. Counterevidence abounds. Stephen Hawking, for example, confined to a wheelchair by Lou Gehrig's disease, lacks a good number of sensorimotor abilities but clearly has no problem forging new understanding.

29 Harding, *Is Science Multicultural?*, 64.

30 Haraway, "Situated Knowledges," 592.

31 Ibid., 596.

Bibliography

Abram, David. *The Spell of the Sensuous*. New York: Vintage, 1996.

Alcoff, Linda, and Elizabeth Potter, eds. *Feminist Epistemologies*. New York: Routledge, 1993.

Allen, Colin, and Marc Beckoff. *Species of Mind: The Philosophy and Biology of Cognitive Ethology*. Cambridge: MIT Press, 1997.

Allen, Paula Gunn. *The Sacred Hoop: Recovering the Feminine in Native American Traditions*. New York: Beacon, 1992.

Aristotle. *The Basic Works of Aristotle*. Edited by R. McKeown. New York: Random House, 1941.

Baier, Annette. *Moral Prejudices: Essays on Ethics*. Cambridge: Harvard University Press, 1999.

Barnes, Barry, David Bloor, and John Henry. *Scientific Knowledge: A Sociological Analysis*. London: Athlone, 1996.

Bass, Rick. *The Book of the Yaak*. Boston: Houghton Mifflin, 1996.

———. "Getting It Right." In *Headwaters*, edited by A. Smith, 5–7. Missoula, Mont.: Hellgate Writers, 1996.

Basso, Keith. "Stalking with Stories." In *On Nature: Nature, Landscape, and Natural History*, edited by D. Halpern, 95–116. San Francisco: North Point Press, 1987.

———. *Wisdom Sits in Places: Landscape and Language among the Western Apache*. Albuquerque: University of New Mexico Press, 1996.

Basso, Keith, and Steven Feld, eds. *Senses of Place*. Santa Fe, N.M.: School of American Research Press, 1996.

Ben-Zeev, A. "The Kantian Revolution in Perception." *Journal for the Theory of Social Behavior* 4 (March 1984): 69–84.

Bigwood, Carol. *Earth Muse: Feminism, Nature, and Art*. Philadelphia: Temple University Press, 1993.

Bleier, Ruth. *Science and Gender: A Critique of Biology and Its Theories on Women*. New York: Pergamon, 1984.

Booth, Annie, and Harvey Jacobs. "Ties That Bind: Native American Beliefs as a Foundation for Environmental Consciousness." *Environmental Ethics* 12 (spring 1990): 27–43.

Borgmann, Albert. *Crossing the Post-Modern Divide*. Chicago: University of Chicago Press, 1998.

Burch, Robert. "On the Ethical Determination of Geography: A Kantian Prolegomena." In *Philosophy and Geography I: Space, Place, and Environmental Ethics*, edited by Andrew Light and Jonathan Smith, 15–47. New York: Rowman and Littlefield, 1997.

Burge, Tyler. "Individualism and the Mental." In *Midwest Studies in Philosophy*, vol. 4, edited by Peter A. French, Theodore E. Uehling Jr., and Howard K. Wettstein, 73–121. Minneapolis: University of Minnesota Press, 1979.

Callicott, J. Baird. "Traditional American Indian and Western Attitudes towards Nature: An Overview." *Environmental Ethics* 4 (winter 1982): 293–318.

Callicott, J. Baird, and Michael P. Nelson. *The Great New Wilderness Debate.* Athens: University of Georgia Press, 1998.

Carnap, Rudolf. "Testability and Meaning." *Philosophy of Science* 3 (1936): 419–471.

Casey, Edward S. *The Fate of Place.* Berkeley: University of California Press, 1997.

———. *Getting Back into Place.* Bloomington: Indiana University Press, 1993.

———. "How to Get from Space to Place in Fairly Short Stretch of Time." In *Senses of Place,* edited by Steven Feld and Keith Basso, 13–52. Santa Fe, N.M.: School of American Research Press, 1996.

Cheney, J. "Post-Modern Environmental Ethics: Ethics as Bioregional Narrative." *Environmental Ethics* 11 (summer 1989): 117–134.

———. "Rivers of Thought: Confluences of Indigenous and Euro-American Philosophies." Paper presented at the Aboriginal Peoples' Conference, 18–20 October 1996 at Lakehead University, Thunder Bay, Ontario.

Church, R. W. *Bacon.* New York: Harper, 1902.

Churchland, Paul. "A Deeper Unity: Some Feyerabendian Themes in Neurocomputational Form." In *Cognitive Models of Science,* edited by Ronald Giere, 341–363. Minnesota Studies in the Philosophy of Science no. 15. Minneapolis: University of Minnesota Press, 1992.

———. *Matter and Consciousness: A Contemporary Introduction to the Philosophy of Mind.* Cambridge: MIT Press, 1984.

———. "To Transform the Phenomena: Feyerabend, Proliferation, and Recurrent Neural Networks." In *The Worst Enemy of Science? Essays in Memory of Paul Feyerabend,* edited by J. Preston, G. Munevar, and D. Lamb, 148–158. New York: Oxford University Press, 2000.

Clark, Andy. *Being There: Putting Brain, Body, and World Together Again.* Cambridge: MIT Press, 1997.

———. "Where Brain, Body and World Collide." *Daedalus* 127 (spring 1998): 257–280.

Cobb, Edith. *The Ecology of Imagination in Childhood.* New York: Columbia University Press, 1977.

Code, Lorraine. *Epistemic Responsibility.* Hanover, N.H.: University Press of New England, 1987.

———. "Taking Subjectivity into Account." In *Feminist Epistemologies,* edited Linda Alcoff and Elizabeth Potter, 15–48. New York: Routledge, 1993.

———. *What Can She Know? Feminist Theory and the Construction of Knowledge.* Ithaca: Cornell University Press, 1991.

———. "What Is Natural about Epistemology Naturalized?" *American Philosophy Quarterly* 33, no. 1 (January 1996): 1–22.

Cordova, Viola. "Eco-Indian: A Response to J. Baird Callicott." *Ayaangwaamizin* 1, no. 1 (1997): 31–44.

Darwin, Charles. *On the Origin of the Species by Natural Selection.* London: Murray, 1859.

Dawkins, Richard. *The Selfish Gene.* New York: Oxford University Press, 1976.

DeLaguna, Frederica. *Under Mount Saint Elias: The History and Culture of the Yakutat Tlingit.* 3 vols. Washington, D.C.: Smithsonian Institution Press, 1972.

Deloria, Vine. *Custer Died for Your Sins: An Indian Manifesto.* Norman: University of Oklahoma Press, 1988.

———. *God Is Red.* Golden, Colo.: Fulcrum, 1994.

Dennett, Daniel. *Darwin's Dangerous Idea: Evolution and the Meanings of Life.* New York: Simon and Schuster, 1995.

Descartes, René. *Selected Philosophical Writings.* Edited and translated by J. Cottingham, R. Stoothoff, and D. Murdoch. Cambridge: Cambridge University Press, 1988.

Dewey, John. *Experience and Nature.* New York: Dover, 1958.

Ewing, A. C. *A Short Commentary on Kant's Critique of Pure Reason.* London: Methuen, 1950.

Feyerabend, Paul. *Against Method.* London: Verso, 1975.

———. *Farewell to Reason.* London: Verso, 1987.

———. *Philosophical Papers.* 2 vols. Cambridge: Cambridge University Press, 1981.

———. *Science in a Free Society.* London: NLB, 1978.

Fuller, Steve. "Epistemology Radically Naturalized: Recovering the Normative, the Experimental, and the Social." In *Cognitive Models of Science,* edited by Ronald Giere, 427–459. Minnesota Studies in the Philosophy of Science no. 15. Minneapolis: University of Minnesota Press, 1992.

Gaard, Greta. "Ecofeminism and Wilderness." *Environmental Ethics* 19 (spring 1997): 5–24.

Gibson, James J. *The Ecological Approach to Visual Perception.* Boston: Houghton Mifflin, 1979.

———. *The Perception of the Visual World.* Boston: Houghton Mifflin, 1950.

Giere, Ronald, ed. *Cognitive Models of Science.* Minnesota Studies in the Philosophy of Science no. 15. Minneapolis: University of Minnesota Press, 1992.

———. *Explaining Science: A Cognitive Approach.* Chicago: University of Chicago Press, 1988.

Glotfelty, Cheryll, and Harold Fromm, eds. *The Ecocriticism Reader.* Athens: University of Georgia Press, 1996.

Gould, Stephen J. *The Mismeasure of Man.* New York: W. W. Norton, 1981.

Hacking, Ian. *Representing and Intervening.* Cambridge: Cambridge University Press, 1983.

Hanson, Norwood R. *Patterns of Discovery.* Cambridge: Cambridge University Press, 1958.

Haraway, Donna J. *Modest_Witness@Second_Millennium.FemaleMan©_Meets_Onco Mouse™*. New York: Routledge, 1997.

―――. *Simians, Cyborgs, and Women: The Reinvention of Nature*. New York: Routledge, 1991.

―――. "Situated Knowledges: The Science Question in Feminism and the Privilege of Partial Perspective." *Feminist Studies* 14 no. 3 (fall 1988): 575–599.

Harding, Sandra. *Is Science Multicultural? Postcolonialisms, Feminisms, and Epistemologies*. Bloomington: Indiana University Press, 1998.

―――. "Rethinking Standpoint Epistemology: What Is Strong Objectivity?" In *Feminist Epistemologies*, edited by Linda Alcoff and Elizabeth Potter, 49–82. Bloomington: Indiana University Press, 1993.

―――. *The Science Question in Feminism*. Ithaca: Cornell University Press, 1986.

―――. " 'Strong Objectivity': A Response to the New Objectivity Question." *Synthese* 14 (1995): 331–349.

Hartsock, Nancy. "The Feminist Standpoint: Developing the Ground for a Specifically Feminist Historical Materialism." In *Discovering Reality: Feminist Perspectives on Epistemology, Metaphysics, Methodology, and Philosophy of Science*, edited by Sandra Harding and Merrill Hintikka, 283–311. Dordrecht, Netherlands: Reidel/Kluwer, 1983.

Hayles, Katherine. "Searching for Common Ground." In *Reinventing Nature*, edited by G. Lease and M. Soulé, 47–64. Washington, D.C.: Island Press, 1995.

Held, R., and A. Hein, "Adaptation of Disarranged Hand-Eye Coordination Contingent upon Re-Afferent Stimulation." *Perceptual Motor Skills* 8 (1958): 87–90.

Hesse, Mary. "Need a Constructed Reality be Non-Objective? Reflections on Science and Society." In *The End of Science? Attack and Defense*, edited by Richard Q. Elvee, 53–61. Lanham, Md.: University Press of America, 1992.

Hesse, Mary, and Michael Arbib. *The Construction of Reality*. London: Cambridge University Press, 1986.

Hubbard, Ruth, Mary Sue Henefin, and Barbara Fried, eds. *Women Look at Biology Looking at Women*. Boston: G. K. Hall, 1979.

Hume, David. *An Enquiry Concerning Human Understanding*. Edited by L. A. Selby-Bigge. Oxford: Clarendon Press, 1957.

―――. *A Treatise of Human Nature*, 2nd ed. Edited by L. A. Selby-Bigge and P. Nidditch. Oxford: Clarendon Press, 1978.

Hutchins, Edward. *Cognition in the Wild*. Cambridge: MIT Press, 1995.

Jackendoff, Ray. *Consciousness and the Computational Mind*. Cambridge: MIT Press, 1987.

Jackson, Wes. *Becoming Native to This Place*. Washington, D.C.: Counterpoint, 1996.

Jenness, Diamond. *The Ojibwa Indians of Parry Island: Their Social and Religious Life*. Ottawa: Canadian Department of Mines, 1935.

Johnson, Mark. *The Body in the Mind*. Chicago: University of Chicago Press, 1987.

———. *Moral Imagination: Implications of Cognitive Science for Ethics.* Chicago: University of Chicago Press, 1993.

Johnson, Mark, and George Lakoff. *The Metaphors We Live By.* Chicago: University of Chicago Press, 1980.

Kant, Immanuel. *The Critique of Pure Reason.* Translated by Norman Kemp Smith. New York: St. Martin's Press, 1965.

Knorr-Cetina, Karin. "The Couch, the Cathedral, and the Laboratory: On the Relationship between Experiment and Laboratory in Science." In *Science as Practice and Culture,* edited by Andrew Pickering, 113–138. Chicago: University of Chicago, 1992.

———. "Laboratory Studies: The Cultural Approach." In *Handbook of Science and Technology Studies,* edited by S. Jasanoff, G. Markle, J. Peterson, and T. Pinch, 140–166. London: Sage, 1995.

———. *The Manufacture of Knowledge: An Essay on the Constructivist and Contextual Nature of Science.* Oxford: Pergamon, 1981.

Kuhn, Thomas. *The Structure of Scientific Revolutions.* 2nd ed. Chicago: University of Chicago Press, 1970.

Lakoff, George, and Mark Johnson. *Philosophy in the Flesh: The Embodied Mind and Its Challenge to Western Thought.* New York: Basic Books, 1999.

Latour, Bruno. "Give Me a Laboratory and I Will Raise the World." In *Science Observed: Perspectives on the Social Study of Science,* edited by K. Knorr-Cetina and M. Mulkay, 141–170. London: Sage, 1983.

———. *Pandora's Hope: Essays on the Reality of Science Studies.* Cambridge: Harvard University Press, 1999.

———. *The Pasteurization of France.* Translated by A. Sheridan and J. Law. Cambridge: Harvard University Press, 1988.

Latour, Bruno, and Steve Woolgar. *Laboratory Life: The Social Construction of Scientific Facts.* London: Sage, 1979.

Lenneberg, Eric H. *The Biological Foundations of Language.* New York: Wiley, 1967.

Leopold, Aldo. *A Sand County Almanac: And Sketches Here and There.* Oxford: Oxford University Press, 1987.

Lévi-Strauss, Claude. *The Savage Mind.* Chicago: University of Chicago Press, 1966.

Levins, Richard, and Richard Lewontin. *The Dialectical Biologist.* Cambridge: Harvard University Press, 1985.

Lewontin, Richard. *Biology as Ideology.* New York: Harper Perennial, 1992.

Locke, John. *An Essay Concerning Human Understanding.* Edited by P. Nidditch. Oxford: Oxford University Press, 1975.

Longino, Helen. *Science as Social Knowledge: Values and Objectivity in Science and Social Inquiry.* Princeton: Princeton University Press, 1990.

———. "Subjects, Power, and Knowledge: Description and Prescription in Feminist Philosophies of Science." In *Feminist Epistemologies,* edited by Linda Alcoff and Elizabeth Potter, 101–120. New York: Routledge, 1993.

Lopez, Barry. *The Rediscovery of North America.* New York: First Vintage, 1992.

Mace, William. "James J. Gibson's Strategy for Perceiving: Ask Not What's Inside Your Head, But What Your Head's Inside Of." In *Perceiving, Acting, and Knowing,* edited by R. E. Shaw and J. Bransford, 43–65. Hillsdale: Lawrence Erlbaum, 1977.

Malthus, Thomas. *Essay on the Principles of Population.* Ann Arbor: University of Michigan Press, 1959.

Mann, Bonnie. "World Alienation in Feminist Thought: The Sublime Epistemology of Emphatic Anti-Essentialism." Unpublished article.

Merchant, Carolyn. *The Death of Nature.* New York: Harper and Row, 1980.

Miles, F. A., and J. Wallman, eds. *Visual Motion and Its Role in the Stabilization of Gaze.* Reviews of Oculomotor Research, vol. 5. New York: Elsevier, 1993.

Mill, John Stuart. *On Liberty.* Indianapolis: Hackett, 1978.

Muir, John. *The Story of My Boyhood and Youth.* New York: Houghton Mifflin, 1913.

———. *The Wilderness Journeys.* Edinburgh: Canongate Classics, 1996.

Nagel, Thomas. *A View from Nowhere.* Oxford: Oxford University Press, 1986.

Nelson, Lynn Hankinson. *Who Knows: From Quine to a Feminist Epistemology.* Philadelphia: Temple University Press, 1990.

Nersessian, Nancy. "A Cognitive-Historical Approach to Meaning in Scientific Theories." In *The Process of Science,* edited by Nancy Nersessian, 161–178. Dordrecht, Netherlands: Martinus Nijhoff, 1986.

———. "How Do Scientists Think? Capturing the Dynamics of Conceptual Change in Science." In *Cognitive Models of Science,* edited by Ronald N. Giere, 3–44. Minnesota Studies in the Philosophy of Science no. 15. Minneapolis: University of Minnesota Press, 1992.

Paul, Sherman. "From 'Here/Now': Mostly on Place." In *On Nature's Terms,* edited by Thomas Lyon and Peter Stine, 116–122. College Station: Texas A&M Press, 1992.

Piaget, Jean, and E. W. Beth. *Mathematical Epistemology and Psychology.* Translated by W. Mays. Boston: Reidel, 1966.

Pickering, Andrew. *The Mangle of Practice.* Chicago: University of Chicago, 1995.

Plato. *Collected Dialogues of Plato.* Edited by Edith Hamilton and Huntington Cairns. Princeton: Princeton University Press, 1961.

———. *Phaedrus.* Translated and edited by A. Nehemas and P. Woodruff. Indianapolis: Hackett, 1995.

———. *Symposium.* Translated and edited by A. Nehemas and P. Woodruff. Indianapolis: Hackett, 1989.

Plumwood, Val. *Feminism and the Mastery of Nature.* London: Routledge, 1993.

Preston, Christopher J. "Environment and Belief: The Importance of Place in the Construction of Knowledge." *Ethics and the Environment* 4, no. 2 (1999): 211–218.

Proctor, Robert. *Racial Hygiene: Medicine under the Nazis.* Cambridge: Harvard University Press, 1988.

Putnam, Hilary. "Meaning and Reference." *Journal of Philosophy* 70 (1979): 73–121.

Pylyshyn, Zenon. *Computation and Cognition: Towards a Foundation for Cognitive Science.* Cambridge: MIT Press, 1984.

Quine, Willard V. O. *From a Logical Point of View.* Cambridge: Harvard University Press, 1953.

———. *Ontological Relativity and Other Essays.* New York: Columbia University Press, 1969.

———. *The Roots of Reference.* La Salle, Ill.: Open Court, 1981.

———. *Word and Object.* Cambridge: MIT Press, 1960.

Reed, Edward S. *Encountering the World.* Oxford: Oxford University Press, 1996.

———. *James J. Gibson and the Psychology of Perception,* New Haven: Yale University Press, 1988.

Reed, Edward, and Rebecca Jones. "Gibson's Theory of Perception: A Case of Hasty Epistemologizing?" *Philosophy of Science* 45 (1978): 519–530.

———. "James Gibson's Ecological Revolution in Psychology." *Philosophy of Social Science* 9 (1979): 189–201.

Rehmann-Sutter, Christophe. "Genes in Labs: Concepts of Development and the Standard Environment." Unpublished article.

Rolston, Holmes, III. *Conserving Natural Value.* New York: Columbia University Press, 1994.

———. *Environmental Ethics: Duties to and Values in the Natural World.* Philadelphia: Temple University Press, 1988.

———. "Why Species Matter." In *The Environmental Ethics and Policy Book,* 2nd ed., edited by D. Van De Veer and C. Pierce, 504–511. Belmont, Calif.: Wadsworth, 1998.

Rorty, Richard. *Philosophy and the Mirror of Nature.* Princeton: Princeton University Press, 1979.

———. *Truth and Progress.* Philosophical Papers, vol. 3. Cambridge: Cambridge University Press, 1998.

Rosch, Eleanor. "Principles of Categorization." In *Cognition and Categorization,* edited by Eleanor Rosch and B. Lloyd. Hillsdale, N.J.: Lawrence Erlbaum, 1978.

Roszak, Theodore, Mary E. Gomes, and Allen D. Kanner, eds. *Ecopsychology: Restoring the Earth, Healing the Mind.* San Francisco: Sierra Books, 1995.

Rouse, Joseph. "What Are Cultural Studies of Scientific Knowledge?" *Configurations* 1, no. 1 (1993): 57–94.

Rowlands, Mark. *The Body in Mind.* Cambridge: Cambridge University Press, 1999.

———. *The Environmental Crisis.* New York: St. Martin's Press, 2000.

Russet, Cynthia. *Sexual Science: The Victorian Construction of Womanhood.* Cambridge: Harvard University Press, 1989.

Sack, David. *Homo Geographicus.* Baltimore: Johns Hopkins University Press, 1997.

Schlick, Morris. "On the Foundation of Knowledge." In *Epistemology: The Classic Readings,* edited by David E. Cooper, 242–260. Oxford: Oxford University Press, 1999.

Segall, Marshall, Donald Campbell, and Melville Herskovits, eds. *The Influence of Culture on Visual Perception*. Indianapolis: Bobbs-Merrill, 1966.

Shadish, William R., and Steve Fuller, eds. *The Social Psychology of Science*. New York: Guilford Press, 1994.

Shepard, Paul. *Nature and Madness*. Athens: University of Georgia Press, 1998.

———. "On Animal Friends." In *The Biophilia Hypothesis*, edited by Stephen Kellert and Edward Wilson, 275–300. Washington, D.C.: Island Press, 1993.

———. "Place in American Culture." *North American Review* 262 (fall 1977): 22–32.

Slovic, Scott. "Nature Writing and Environmental Psychology." In *The Ecocriticism Reader*, edited by Cheryll Glotfelty and Harold Fromm, 351–370. Athens: University of Georgia Press, 1996.

Smith, Dorothy. *The Everyday World as Problematic: A Feminist Sociology*. Boston: Northeastern University Press, 1987.

Snyder, Gary. *The Real Work: Interviews and Talks (1964–1979)*. New York: New Directions Books, 1980.

Stephan, Nancy. *The Idea of Race in Science: Great Britain (1800–1960)*. London: Macmillan, 1982.

Thagard, Paul. *Computational Philosophy of Science*. Cambridge: MIT Press, 1988.

———. "Concepts and Conceptual Change." *Synthese* 82 (1990): 255–274.

Tuan, Yi-Fu. *Space and Place: The Perspective of Experience*. Minneapolis: University of Minnesota Press, 1977.

———. *Topophilia: A Study of Environmental Perception, Attitudes, and Values*. Englewood, N.J.: Prentice Hall, 1974.

Tuana, Nancy. "Material Locations." In *Engendering Rationalities*, edited by N. Tuana and S. Morgan, 221–243. Albany: SUNY Press, 2001.

Turnbull, Colin. *The Forest People*. London: Chatto and Windus, 1961.

Varela, Francisco, Evan Thompson, and Eleanor Rosch, eds. *The Embodied Mind: Cognitive Science and Human Experience*. Cambridge: MIT Press, 1991.

Warren, Karen. "The Power and Promise of Ecological Feminism." *Environmental Ethics* 12 (summer 1990): 125–146.

Williams, Terry T. *An Unspoken Hunger*. New York: Vintage, 1994.

Wittgenstein, Ludwig. *Tractatus Logico-Philosophicus*. Ithaca: Cornell University Press, 1971.

Zilman, Adrienne. "Gathering Stories for Hunting Human Nature." *Feminist Studies* 11 (1985): 364–377.

Index

cognition, 70, 73–74; and categorization, 65–66, 72; and dialectical biology, 55–57, 66–67; and the embodied mind, 31, 33, 115, 125–26, 145 (n. 28); and enactivism, 29–35, 65, 74; environmentalist model of, 67–69, 74, 144 (n. 17); experiments in, 65–66; and sense of place, xv, 47, 92–93, 100, 102, 115–16. *See also* cognitive science; knowledge formation
cognitive ethology, 113
cognitive science, 27, 36, 50, 70, 125; and cognitivism, 27–29, 34, 56. *See also* cognition
cognitivism, 27–29, 34, 56, 57. *See also* naturalization, of epistemology
communication, and diversity, 127–28
consumption patterns, xii–xiii
coping mechanisms, mental, 12, 15. *See also* skepticism
cosmogenesis, 77–78. *See also* Plato
creation. *See* cosmogenesis
Critique of Pure Reason, The (Kant), 16
cultural geography, 74–75, 84, 86, 97–99, 107–8
cultural naturalization. *See* naturalization, of epistemology

Darwin, Charles, 22, 25, 27, 29, 50–51, 66. *See also* dialectical biology; evolution
Dawkins, Richard, 52
Deloria, Vine, Jr., 81, 84–88
Dennett, Daniel, 113–14
Descartes, René, 80, 114, 119; and dualism, 12–13, 23, 29, 57–58, 68, 111, 137 (n. 5); and ideas, 8–9, 56, 58–59, 74; *Meditations,* 11, 68, 137 (n. 5); and skepticism, 10–11, 13–14, 20
detachment, 5–7, 8, 10, 14, 107. *See also* transcendence
Dewey, John, 127–28, 130

dialectical biology, 50–53, 54, 74, 97, 107; and cognition, 55–57, 66–67; and visual perception, 60–61
dislocating experience, 89–93, 95–96, 97, 132, 143 (n. 30)
diversity: cultural, 129–30, 133; ecological, 110; and knowledge formation, 119–25; naturalistic argument for, 124–28, 130; philosophy of science argument for, 120–22; of place, 71–72, 117, 119–20, 128–30, 132–34, 144 (n. 1), 145 (n. 27); sociology of science argument for, 122–24
doubt, 10–11. *See also* skepticism
dualism, 12–13, 29, 57–58, 68, 111, 136, 137 (n. 5); between nature and reason, 3, 5, 113–14, 136. *See also* Descartes, René
dynamic Kantianism, 31, 33

ecological diversity, 110
ecological psychology, 57–61, 62–65, 74, 88. *See also* Gibson, James J.
ecological theory, 54
ecopsychology, 2, 71
embodied action, 30, 33–34, 56, 58, 66
embodied imagination, 126–28, 130–32, 145 (n. 28)
embodied mind, 31, 33, 115, 125–26, 145 (n. 28)
empirical psychology, 21, 23
empiricism, 8. *See also* Locke, John
enactivism, 29–34, 43, 49–50, 57, 63, 65–66, 71, 72, 74, 125. *See also* naturalization, of epistemology
environment: and cognition, 63–65, 75, 96–97; and epistemology, 26, 36; and knowledge formation, 30, 34–35, 39–41, 43–46, 49, 71–72, 75–76, 88, 98, 101; organism interaction with, 50–57, 60, 62, 66, 69–72, 108; and perception, 94–95, 97; and visual perception, 58–61. *See also* place

environmental determinism, 96–98, 101, 106

environmental philosophy, 2, 110–11; development of, xiii–xiv, 118–19, 141 (n. 6); and epistemology, 76, 135

environmental possibilism, 98, 101, 107

environmentalism, xiii, xiv, 105, 119

environmentalist model of cognition (Rowlands), 67–69, 74, 144 (n. 17). *See also* cognition

epistemic location, 38, 40, 42, 104, 105, 108. *See also* physical location

epistemology: and anthropocentrism, xi–xii, 105–6, 107, 110, 135–36; and cognitive science, 27; development of, 3–4, 6–9, 13–24, 31, 50, 88–89, 117; and dialectical biology, 55; and ecological psychology, 62–63, 64; and environmental philosophy, 76; and exploitative worldview, 73–74; feminist theory in, 33, 103–5, 106, 108; and natural diversity, 119–20; postmodern, xi, xii, 49, 56, 71, 104, 105, 109, 110; and sense of place, 99, 102; and skepticism, 10–13, 15, 18; and sociological study, 37–41; and the theory-dependence of observation thesis, 94–96; trends in, xii–xiii, 41–42. *See also* modernism, in philosophy; naturalization, of epistemology

Erasmus, 10

ethics, 110–14. *See also* environmental philosophy

evolution, 34, 51–53, 55, 64, 66, 96, 97, 113–14. *See also* Darwin, Charles

evolutionary biology, 50, 57, 68, 102. *See also* dialectical biology

Ewing, A. C., 16

experience, sensory: and knowledge formation, 8, 15–17, 19–23, 24, 30, 31, 55, 61

extended mind, 69

externalism, 67–69, 70, 116

feminist theory, 37, 71, 112–13, 122–23; in epistemology, 33, 103–5, 106, 108

Feyerabend, Paul K., 36–37, 42, 120–22, 123, 125, 126

forms: conversion of, into ideas, 8–9, 10, 13; knowledge of, 5, 7–8, 77–78, 79. *See also* Plato

Gaard, Greta, 91, 142 (n. 25)

geography, 1–2; cultural, 74–75, 84, 86, 97–99, 107–8; sacred, 86–88

Gibson, James J., 57–59, 60, 61, 62–63, 64, 66, 68, 140 (n. 16). *See also* visual perception

Gould, Stephen J., 37, 103

Hanson, Norwood Russel, 94

Haraway, Donna, 41, 122–23, 126, 136, 143 (n. 10)

Harding, Sandra, 38, 108–10, 122, 123, 126, 128–29, 130, 135–36

Hayles, N. Katherine, 33

Heracleitus, 10

Herbert (robot), 69–70

Hesse, Mary, 31

hidden subjectivities, 38. *See also* bias

historical cultural naturalization. *See* naturalization, of epistemology

history: and sacred geography, 86; of science, 36–37, 74, 121–22

Hume, David, 10–12, 15, 18, 20, 21–22, 111. *See also* skepticism

Huntingdon, Ellsworth, 96

Hutchins, Ed, 44, 48, 72, 107

idealism, 17, 39–40

ideas, 11–13, 15, 28, 56, 58–59, 74; alienation of, from the physical world, 13–14, 18, 119; conversion of forms into, 8–9, 10, 13 image schemas. *See* schemas

imagination, embodied, 126–28, 130–32, 145 (n. 28)

indigenous cultures, and sense of place, 80–88, 109, 110, 133

instrumental values. *See* values, natural

intrinsic values. *See* values, natural

Jackson, Wes, xiv

Jenness, Diamond, 80–81

Johnson, Mark, 31–34, 48, 49, 56, 71, 72, 115, 125–28, 130, 132

Kant, Immanuel, 31, 33, 39, 42, 94, 111; *The Critique of Pure Reason*, 16; and skepticism, 14–18, 20, 22–23, 25–26, 29

Knorr-Cetina, Karin, 40, 41, 43–44, 45, 49, 72

knowledge formation, 3, 9–11, 29; and abstraction, 5–6, 10, 13, 17, 80; and the body, 7–8, 14; and categories of localness, 108; and dialectical biology, 55; and diversity, 119–25; and the environment, 30, 34–35, 39–41, 43–46, 49, 71–72, 75–76, 88, 96–98, 101; and experience, 15–17, 19–20, 22–23; and perception, 57–63, 64–66; and reason, 5–6, 8–9, 22; and schemas, 30–34; scientific, 36–37, 39, 40, 109; and sensorimotor activity, 30–35, 65–66, 69, 130–32; and sensory experience, 8, 15–17, 19–23, 24, 30, 31, 55, 61; and the verifiability principle, 18–19. *See also* belief formation; cognition; richly situated knowledge; situated knowledge

Kuhn, Thomas, 36, 37, 42

lab studies. *See* naturalization, of epistemology

Lakoff, George, 32, 33

language, 36, 63, 70, 105, 111, 115–16

Latour, Bruno, 13, 14, 17, 23, 29, 40, 43, 49, 72

Lenneberg, Eric H., 70

Leopold, Aldo, xiv

Levins, Richard, 50, 51, 52–56, 57. *See also* dialectical biology

Lévi-Strauss, Claude, 70

Lewontin, Richard, 50, 51, 52–56, 57. *See also* dialectical biology

location, epistemic, 38, 40, 42, 104, 105, 108

location, physical, 73, 83, 92, 97, 107–8, 129–30. *See also* place

Locke, John: and ideas, 8–10, 11, 15, 56, 58–59; and skepticism, 20–21, 23

logical positivism, 18–21, 23, 28, 56

logics of colonization, 112. *See also* Plumwood, Val

logos, 78. *See also* *chora*

Longino, Helen, 123–24, 129

Lopez, Barry, 118

Luther, Martin, 10

Mach, Ernest, 20

Mann, Bonnie, 106

materialistic cultural naturalization. *See* naturalization, of epistemology

material-semiotic order of nature, 41

Meditations (Descartes), 11, 68, 137 (n. 5)

metaphysical deduction, 16. *See also* Kant, Immanuel

Mill, John Stuart, 120–22, 127

mind: cognitivism and, 27–28; and ideas, 11, 15–16; separation of, from the body, 8, 14–15, 29, 34, 68, 137 (n. 5); separation of, from the world, 14–18, 22–23, 28–29, 43, 48, 58. *See also* brain; place and mind connection

"mind-mind problem," 28. *See also* cognitivism

modernism, in philosophy, 8–9, 10, 29, 42, 49, 58, 61, 107; and Christianity, 14;

passive mind viewpoint of the, 22, 35; and representationalism, 55; and skepticism, 11–13, 15, 18–19, 28. *See also* postmodernism, in philosophy

morality, 112; connection of, to land, 81–84, 85–86, 88, 98, 135

Muir, John, 47, 89

myopia, among Inuits, 96

Nagel, Thomas, 33

Native Americans: cultural studies of, 81–85, 142 (n. 17); religious beliefs of, 85–88

naturalization, of epistemology, 21–23, 55, 74, 107, 134; cultural, 26, 35–40, 41–42, 65, 71, 75, 125; materialistic (lab studies), 40–45, 49, 72, 88; scientific, 26–35, 39, 42, 75, 125

nature: destruction of, 112, 135; material-semiotic order of, 41; neglect of, in epistemology, 106–7; preservation of, 117; reason and, 3, 5, 113–14, 136; separation of, from artificial environments, 75–76; values found in, 114–16, 117, 135. *See also* place

Nehemas, Alexander, 79–80

Neurath, Otto, 20

Newton, Isaac, 15, 80

objectivity, 122–23, 125–26

optic array. *See* array, optic and ambient

Pasteur, Louis, 43

Patterson, Dudley, 81–84, 86. *See also* Basso, Keith; Western Apache

Paul, Sherman, 1

perception: and assumptions, 94, 99; and dislocating experiences, 90–93, 143 (n. 30); and environment, 94–95, 97; and knowledge formation, 57–63, 64–66; and place, 90–93, 96; visual, 57–65

perceptual orienteering, 91. *See also* dislocating experience

Phaedo (Socrates), 6

Phaedrus (Plato), 6, 78–80, 88, 89

philosophy, environmental. *See* environmental philosophy

philosophy of science, 120–22, 125. *See also* diversity

philosophy of the mind, 67–68, 70. *See also* environmental philosophy

physical location, 73, 83, 92, 97, 107–8, 129–30. *See also* epistemic location; place

physical world, alienation from ideas, 13–14, 15, 18, 106–7, 119. *See also* environment

physiology, 96–97

Piaget, Jean, 30–31, 33, 46, 49

Pickering, Andrew, 39–41, 44, 49, 71, 72, 75, 106, 134, 141 (n. 3)

place: and belief formation, 81, 98–99; diversity of, 71–72, 117, 119, 128–30, 132–34, 144 (n. 1), 145 (n. 27); as opposed to space, 74–75, 141 (n. 4); and perception, 90–93, 96; and physiology, 96–97; and wisdom, 81–83, 84. *See also* environment; place and mind connection; sense of place

place and mind connection, 2, 4, 24, 47–48, 73, 99, 101–2, 109, 116–17, 136; and environmental philosophy, 110; and environmental policy, 119, 128, 133

Plato, 3–4, 7–8, 10, 62, 111, 137 (n. 5); forms of, 5, 7–8, 13, 77–78, 79; influence of, in philosophy, 22, 28, 29, 35, 42, 119; and sense of place *(chora)*, 77–80, 88; and truth, 5–6, 7. Works: *Phaedrus*, 6, 78–80, 88, 89; *Republic*, 6; *Theaetetus*, 57, 74; *Timaeus*, 5, 77–78, 88. *See also* Western philosophy

Plumwood, Val, 112–13, 114

policy, environmental, 119, 132, 136

10; and truth versus rhetoric,
3–4
space, 137 (n. 1); as opposed to place,
74–75, 141 (n. 4). See also *chora*
Stephan, Nancy, 37–38
subjectivities, hidden, 38, 103–4, 108,
122–23, 143 (n. 3). *See also* bias
supercategories. *See* categories of
localness, supercategories
synaesthetic participation, 83–84
systemic values. *See* values, natural

tensions, between cultural and scientific
naturalizers, 35–36, 48, 75, 134–36
Theaetetus (Plato), 57, 74
theory-dependence of observation
thesis, 94–96, 121
Thomas Aquinas, Saint, 8
Thompson, Evan, 27, 29, 30, 49, 55, 65
thought processes. *See* knowledge
formation
Timaeus (Plato), 5, 77–78, 88
Tractatus (Wittgenstein), 18–19
transcendence, 14, 23, 42, 70, 73–74, 97,
121
transperspectivity, 126–27
truth, 3–6, 8, 9, 22
Tuan, Yi-Fu, 74, 93, 98–99, 141 (n. 4)
Tuana, Nancy, 106

Turnbull, Colin, 93
twin earth thought experiment, 67. *See
also* externalism

value bias. *See* bias
values, natural, 114–16, 117, 135
Varela, Francisco, 27, 29, 30, 49, 55, 65
verifiability principle, 18–20. *See also*
logical positivism
visual perception, 57–63; and cognition,
64–65. *See also* perception

Warren, Karen, 112
Western Apache, 81–84, 88, 107, 109, 135.
See also Basso, Keith; Patterson,
Dudley
Western philosophy, xiii–xiv, 2–3, 7–8,
74, 111, 113; and the idea of place,
76–80, 97
Whitehead, Alfred North, 4
Williams, Terry Tempest, 73
Winter, Stephen, 126
wisdom, 81–83, 84
Wittgenstein, Ludwig Josef Johan, 18–19
Woodruff, Paul, 79–80
Woolgar, Steve, 40

Zihlman, Adrienne, 37